King Caesar of Duxbury

Exploring the World of Ezra Weston, Shipbuilder & Merchant

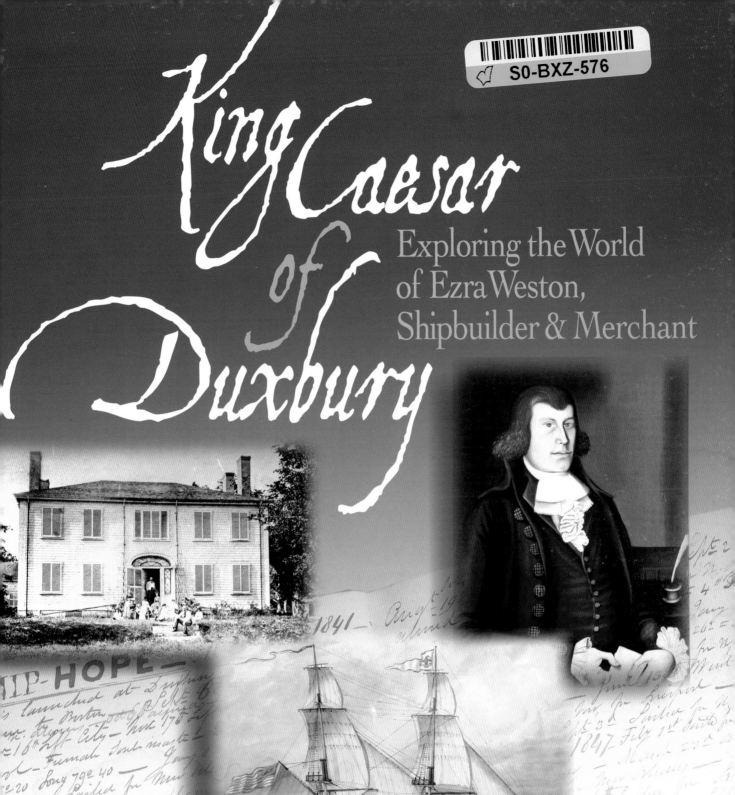

Patrick T. J. Browne

Published by the

DUXBURY
RURAL & HISTORICAL
SOCIETY, INC.

479 Washington Street, P.O. Box 2865
Duxbury, Massachusetts 02331
781-934-6106; Fax 781-934-5730
www.duxburyhistory.org

Printed in the United States of America.
ISBN # 0-941859-10-X

Library of Congress Cataloging-in-Publication Data

Browne, Patrick T.J.

King Caesar of Duxbury : exploring the world of Ezra Weston, shipbuilder and merchant
     p. cm.

ISBN 0-941859-10-X

1. Weston, Ezra, 1772-1842. 2. Weston family. 3. Shipbuilding industry--Massachusetts--Duxbury--History.
4. Merchant marine--Massachusetts--Duxbury--History. 5. Duxbury (Mass.)--Biography. I. Title.

VK140.W356B85 2006

338.7'623820092--dc22   2005029290

Table of Contents

The doorway of the King Caesar
House c. 1900. The woman
is a member of the Knapp family.
On the step sits the billet head
of King Caesar's brig **Ceres**,
launched in 1828.

Weston Family Genealogy

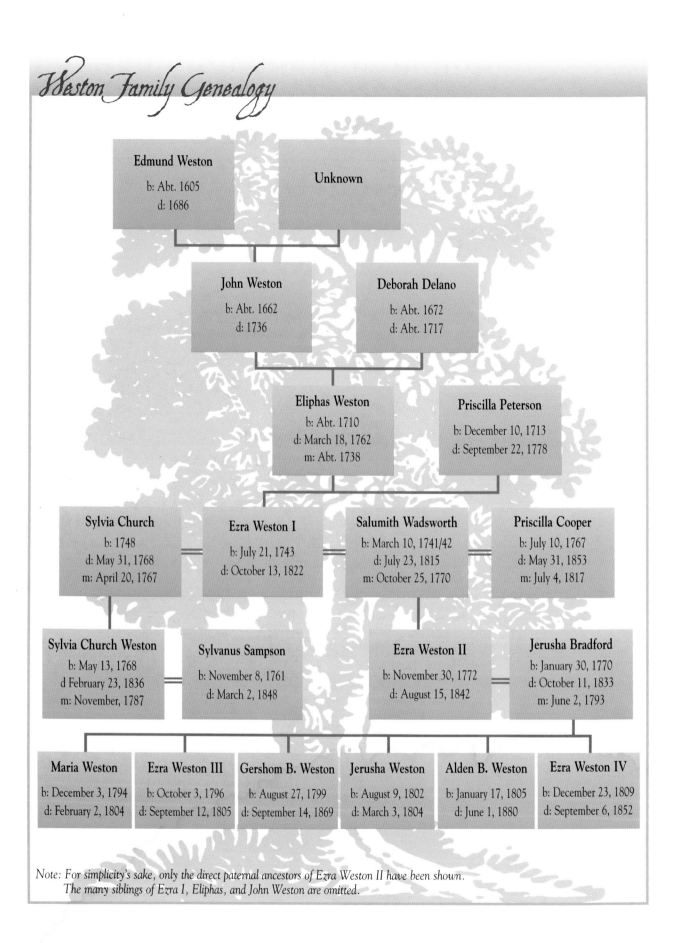

Edmund Weston
b: Abt. 1605
d: 1686

Unknown

John Weston
b: Abt. 1662
d: 1736

Deborah Delano
b: Abt. 1672
d: Abt. 1717

Eliphas Weston
b: Abt. 1710
d: March 18, 1762
m: Abt. 1738

Priscilla Peterson
b: December 10, 1713
d: September 22, 1778

Sylvia Church
b: 1748
d: May 31, 1768
m: April 20, 1767

Ezra Weston I
b: July 21, 1743
d: October 13, 1822

Salumith Wadsworth
b: March 10, 1741/42
d: July 23, 1815
m: October 25, 1770

Priscilla Cooper
b: July 10, 1767
d: May 31, 1853
m: July 4, 1817

Sylvia Church Weston
b: May 13, 1768
d February 23, 1836
m: November, 1787

Sylvanus Sampson
b: November 8, 1761
d: March 2, 1848

Ezra Weston II
b: November 30, 1772
d: August 15, 1842

Jerusha Bradford
b: January 30, 1770
d: October 11, 1833
m: June 2, 1793

Maria Weston
b: December 3, 1794
d: February 2, 1804

Ezra Weston III
b: October 3, 1796
d: September 12, 1805

Gershom B. Weston
b: August 27, 1799
d: September 14, 1869

Jerusha Weston
b: August 9, 1802
d: March 3, 1804

Alden B. Weston
b: January 17, 1805
d: June 1, 1880

Ezra Weston IV
b: December 23, 1809
d: September 6, 1852

Note: For simplicity's sake, only the direct paternal ancestors of Ezra Weston II have been shown. The many siblings of Ezra I, Eliphas, and John Weston are omitted.

Acknowledgments

This book, particularly the research that went into it, has been a group effort. The transcription of documents and entry of volumes of fleet data into several computer databases required many, many hours of work on behalf of numerous people to whom I am greatly indebted. The data entry from two of the most important sources on the affairs of the Weston Fleet (Ezra Weston's Vessel Memorandum Book and Cargo Book) was completed by Linda Pisani after months of work. Jean Kennett spent an equal amount of time in entering data on vessels built in Duxbury and imports to Liverpool. Both also transcribed ship registers of the district of Plymouth aided by Duxbury High School students Michael McKinley, Zach McMann, Phillippe Moitino, and Kenny Flynn.

Knapp family outside the King Caesar House c. 1915.

Letters and journals were transcribed by Sally Forrest, Page Brown, Patricia Flaherty, Doug Milne, and Carol Todd. Other research assistance was provided by Jordie Saucerman, Kristin Hall, Michael Markowicz, and Marc Ewart and I thank them for their support. I am indebted to my father, Gerald Browne, for many things of course, but most pertinently for his help in transcribing several ship's logs kept by King Caesar's captains.

For supplying information on the Weston family, I'd like to thank William Bradford Drury, Bradford Weston III, Robert and Donald Severy and especially Marjorie and Richard Winslow for their crucial help in this project.

Historians Rebecca Robinson and Bonnie Smith were kind enough to share information and research related to Boston commerce and merchants for which I am grateful.

My thanks go to fellow members of the Duxbury Rural and Historical Society staff, Sarah Gallagher and Alison Arnold, who were so helpful in holding down the fort while I was in the thick of research and writing.

For their help in obtaining documents and photographs, I'd like to thank Walter Hickey of the National Archives and Records Administration, Holly Smith and Chris Carden of the Bostonian Society, Megan Friedel and Kim Nusco of the Massachusetts Historical Society, Michael Lapides of the New Bedford Whaling Museum, Christine Michelini of the Peabody Essex Museum, Judy Sime, David Murphy and Elaine Winquist of the Duxbury Free Library, and particularly Jonathan Lane of the American Antiquarian Society who located several gems of newspaper articles related to King Caesar.

Thanks, as well, to the folks at Kiskadee Coffee in Plymouth. It's a great place to write a book.

When the time came for editing and design, I relied completely on the skill and expertise of the DRHS Publications Committee ably chaired by William McArdle. My thanks to the committee for all their hard work. I very much appreciate the editing and fact-checking provided by Katherine Pillsbury, Robert Hale, Tony Kelso, Alice Vautrain, Norman Forgit, Jack Pow and Cathy Cantin.

Norm Forgit has done a truly magnificent job with the graphic design. He can, in fact, be credited with first generating the idea that led to this publication. Throughout the process he provided creative suggestions, editorial help, and a much needed nudge from time to time. He is an extremely talented designer and we were fortunate to have his help in this project.

Finally, my thanks to my wife Kelly, who has endless patience for a husband often lost in another century. This couldn't have been written without her support.

PROLOGUE

The Legend

Stepping through tall weeds, Frederick Bradford Knapp took a hard look at the old King Caesar House on an August day in 1886. The building was in tough shape, shuttered, paint peeling. It had rarely seen occupants for the past six years, he was told. Old "King Caesar," the legendary shipbuilder, had been dead more than 40 years. The house now belonged to his grandchildren. They didn't want to keep it.

Knapp, 29 years old and Superintendent of Buildings at Harvard College, walked King Caesar's grounds and inspected the property with an experienced eye. A miniature forest of poplar saplings had taken over the front lawn. The gardens were overgrown and the hedges a disaster. Inside the darkened house sat much of the furniture owned by its last resident who had died six years earlier. King Caesar's middle son, Alden B. Weston, had lived in the house alone, a recluse in his old age. He had been the manager of the E. Weston & Sons counting house. Knapp later found some of the company's old papers tucked away on shelves—dusty, leather-bound ledgers.

There were traces of the old Weston family industry that had closed the year Knapp was born, but all had now fallen into decay. Directly in front of the house, just on the other side of the fence, a huge wharf thrust out into the bay. Stripped of its warehouses and counting rooms, it presented a desolate scene. Knapp was told that a ropewalk, King Caesar's largest building, once stood to the west of the house. The field where it stood was covered with tall grass now. And across the river there, at the base of a gently sloping hillside now dotted with cows, the shipbuilder had launched the largest ships of his day. Behind the house, empty old barns stood in a huddle.

To Knapp, it was perfect.

He and his wife, Fanny Hall Knapp, had spent the better part of that summer searching for an estate on which to establish a preparatory school. Making whirlwind trips both together and separately, they systematically explored rural towns across eastern Massachusetts, seeking aging manors that could be bought cheaply. Many were adequate, but none seemed to have the right combination of qualities. They were either inaccessible, located in unattractive towns, too far from the water, or abutting "not good neighbors."[1]

But the King Caesar estate, despite the decay, would do nicely.

Frederick Bradford Knapp (1857-1932) in 1883. Raised for the most part in Plymouth, Massachusetts, Knapp was a civil engineer and Superintendent of Harvard's Buildings and Grounds before coming to Duxbury.

Knapp bought the property before the month was out.

By the time Knapp acquired the house, it had become the focus of local mythology. Old King Caesar, the legend went, had owned the largest fleet of merchant ships in the country, perhaps even the world. He built them right here in Duxbury, launching them into a shallow harbor in which their keels scraped the mud. King Caesar had everything he needed right in this little town: a shipyard, a farm, a sailcloth mill, a blacksmith shop, and a ropewalk. Even Daniel Webster had said King Caesar was the greatest merchant of the time.[2]

If he didn't know already, Knapp would soon find out that there were actually two King Caesars, father and son.

In 1764, Ezra Weston I (1743-1822) established a small shipyard along Duxbury's marshy shore. His success, his formidable character, and his audacious designs for the community would earn him the nickname "King Caesar." This title passed to his son, Ezra Weston II (1772-1842), who built and lived in the striking mansion now known as the "King Caesar House." Father and son, each having different priorities defined by their times, built up a commercial enterprise that became one of the most important in the Commonwealth and was by far the largest mercantile operation on the shores of Plymouth County in its day.

The Weston firm is rarely included in the annals of New England maritime history. Passing mentions usually cite the claim to fame bestowed on the Westons by Daniel Webster. In a speech delivered in Saratoga, New York, in 1841, Webster said, "I live on the seacoast of New England, and one of our nearest neighbors is the largest ship-owner, probably, in the United States. During the past year he has made what might suffice for two or three fortunes of moderate size."[3]

King Caesar's House c.1883. This earliest known photograph of the home of Ezra Weston II shows the house just after the death of his son, Alden B. Weston. Assembled for the photograph are some of King Caesar's grandchildren and great-grandchildren. The individual seated on the steps in the foreground is believed to be Alden B. Weston II (1844-1919). The man in the doorway is believed to be Gershom B. Weston II (1821-1887), the eldest grandchild. King Caesar's grandchildren used the house only sporadically from 1880-1886.

Certainly the Weston firm was bringing in a great fortune. And its fleet was indeed considerable. In the year when Webster made his observation, the Westons launched the largest merchant ship yet built in New England. The firm operated a fleet of 14 vessels totaling 4,531 tons. Determining whether this was, in fact, the largest fleet afloat in the United States at that time is difficult. But suffice it to say, the Weston fleet was significant.

The title "largest ship-owner" is attached to Weston in a number of histories, including that of Massachusetts historian Henry Howe, who wrote, "Lloyds of London listed more than a hundred ships owned by Ezra Weston, making him one of the largest ship owners in the world." Indeed, the firm built or otherwise acquired at least 110 vessels over the course of three generations. Again, determining whether any American firm surpassed this accomplishment prior to 1850 is difficult and, to some extent, irrelevant. However, gaining an understanding of the scope of the achievements of the Weston family within a greater historical context is key.[4]

The relative absence of the Westons from the history books, aside from offhand mentions such as these, is puzzling. Part of the problem is lack of documentation. Essentially no personal papers survive, so we have little or no insights into King Caesar's personal opinions, family life, or private observations. What do exist are business records. Difficult to decipher and challenging to place in context, the data left by the Westons requires extensive tabulation and analysis. This hurdle was sizeable enough to prevent many from attempting to write about the Westons.

In their history of early 18th-century Massachusetts shipbuilding, historians Bernard and Lotte Bailyn wrote, "A sense of magnitude lies often at the heart of historical understanding. Without realistic notions of scale, without some form of calibration, we cannot answer certain uniquely historical questions of growth and decline and the phasing of change."[5] Establishing this sense of scale and change is essential where the Westons are concerned. First, it is important to establish a basis of comparison for the various mercantile activities on the South Shore. Second, and, perhaps, more important, it is crucial to identify the periods of growth and decline in the Weston firm itself and to seek explanations for them.

Examining the statistics compiled from the Weston business records and other sources on fleet ownership on the South Shore is the best means of establishing this context of growth and change. More than just numbers, the data reveals the basis of the Weston firm's success and their most formidable obstacles. Other sources, some anecdotal, also contribute a sense of time, place, and character. Viewed against the proper backdrop of facts and figures, the legendary King Caesar begins to appear a bit more human. His motives and schemes can, to some extent, be revealed and understood.

For Frederick Knapp's daughters who grew up on the estate, King Caesar would primarily remain a man of legend—the unknowable autocrat.

They probably preferred it that way.

CHAPTER ONE

Ancestors

Edmund Weston

The story of the Weston family of Duxbury begins in London on May 8, 1635. Edmund Weston, age 30, having made the weighty decision to migrate to Boston, registered his name with Richard Cooper, master of the *Elizabeth & Ann*. A week later, the ship sailed with a total of 107 passengers on board. The vessel arrived in Boston sometime in mid-summer.[1]

Of Edmund Weston's origins we know little. According to family tradition, he was a thresher of grain by profession. One genealogist claimed to have traced Weston's origins to either Oxfordshire or Warwickshire, but neither of these assertions can be confirmed.[2]

Disembarking in Boston, Edmund encountered a small, five-year-old town struggling to accommodate a dramatic influx of colonists. In the 1630s, English folk found themselves on the move due to a confluence of various unfortunate circumstances, including plague in the 1620s, a number of poor harvests that caused widespread poverty, and political and religious upheaval. The best solution for many who had been uprooted by misfortune was emigration to the colonies and the promise of free land. In all, approximately 21,000 people made the journey to New England in the 1630s, an influx known as the Great Migration.[3]

It is interesting to note that the progenitor of Duxbury's Weston family represented an exception to the well-known pattern of immigration in New England. In contrast with the colonies in the south, the Puritan colonies were largely settled by families, most of whom came for religious reasons. They were, as historian Francis Bremer observed, "sober rural and urban middle class folk," who came because they had "sense of their own place in God's providential design." They were not financial adventurers like the vast numbers of unmarried men flocking to Virginia.[4]

Edmund Weston, however, did not travel with a family. In fact, many of the passengers (about 36%) on that voyage of the *Elizabeth & Ann* were single men. Why this vessel represents an exception to the more general pattern of immigration, and specifically why an unattached male like Weston chose Boston instead of other more promising destinations for a young man (such as Virginia where the incentive of free land attracted so many laborers) are questions that must go unanswered.[5]

Placing Weston further outside the norm for New England settler is the fact that he appears to have come as an indentured servant, a rarity in Massachusetts as compared to other colonies. Soon after arriving in Boston, Edmund made his way to Plymouth where he first appears in the records on November 2, 1636 as an indentured servant to John Winslow. Weston may have let himself out as a servant to pay for his passage to Boston. Thus, the story of the Weston family is one of poverty to great prosperity over the course of a few generations.[6]

An indentured servant willingly put himself in the service of someone, usually to pay a debt or, in an immigrant's case, to pay for passage. There was also the time-honored practice of "putting out," by which parents indentured their sons as apprentices in a form of vocational schooling. The typical term of servitude was five to seven years. During that time, the master was required to supply food, clothing, and shelter for the servant. The contract usually stipulated some sort of financial reward at the end of the term, often an accrued annual wage or a new suit of clothes and sometimes a grant of land if the master chose to make such an arrangement with the colonial government. Edmund Weston was to receive six bushels of corn and a wage of £6 per year.[7]

The millpond on Stony Brook was created in 1639 upon the construction of Duxbury's first gristmill near where Route 3A today crosses the brook. The land on the opposite shore was part of Edmund Weston's farm.

John Winslow, a greatly respected man of the colony and brother to Edward Winslow, transferred Weston's indenture to Nathaniel Thomas in 1636. It is not clear where Weston lived while he served out his term for the next two years but it was probably close by, if not within, his master's residence in Marshfield.

Upon the completion of his servitude, Weston wasted no time in establishing himself as an industrious member of the colony. On November 4, 1639, he entered into a partnership with John Carew of Marshfield to clear and plant Carew's land. A year later, the colony granted Weston his own land—a four-acre farm on Stony Brook in Duxbury.

Duxbury had been incorporated as a town only two years before in 1637. Prior to that, the colonial leaders had been reluctant to allow separate churches to be established outside of Plymouth. From 1628 to 1637, those who had received land grants in Duxborough, so called, were required to travel to Plymouth each Sabbath "that they better repair to the worship of God." In those early years, Duxbury settlers abandoned their farms in the winter and lived in Plymouth for the colder months in order to avoid a difficult weekly journey. It was an inconvenience and a frustration for those who would have preferred to live on their farms year-round.[8]

Eventually the inhabitants of Duxbury petitioned to be released from the Plymouth church, to establish their own meeting house, and to engage their own minister. At the time of incorporation in 1637 the population numbered 23 families, including several of the colony's most important individuals: Myles Standish, John Alden, and William Brewster among them.

Edmund Weston did not rise to any such position of importance. He was elected a grand juryman and a surveyor of highways, indicating that he was well thought of and upright. Weston apparently worked his farm successfully. He received several additional land grants, including a partnership in the Bridgewater Grant when Duxbury acquired that vast tract in 1649. On June 7, 1653, Weston was granted "freeman" status, obtaining at that time the full right to vote in colonial affairs.[9]

Weston's farm was located west of the Green Harbor Path (part of which is now the northern end of Tremont Street) in the area of Duxbury near the Marshfield line now known as Millbrook. The farm fronted on Stony Brook just west of the millpond. His house, long gone, sat on a knoll near today's Orchard Lane, and his descendants occupied the property for nearly 250 years. Indeed, Weston descendants built numerous houses along Tremont Street, not far from the original homestead.[10]

Edmund Weston apparently married late in life, sometime around 1655. Records do not show his bride's name, although there is a tradition that she might have been a Delano. They had four children, three boys and a girl. For the purposes of our story, we shall focus on the youngest child, born about 1662.

John Weston

On the shore of Morton's Hole, a quiet inlet of Duxbury Bay, on the west side of the peninsula known as the Nook, John Weston began building small sailing vessels around 1690. No doubt they were simple craft, similar to the shallops made during the Pilgrim era. He worked at a sporadic pace, producing no more than one boat per year and, in some years, none at all. He also managed a small farm on the southwest side of Captain's Hill, now the vicinity of Crescent Street.

Shipbuilding in Massachusetts was already a thriving industry toward the end of the 17th century, as evidenced by the vessel registrations compiled by historians Bernard and Lotte Bailyn. Of the 211 vessels registered in Massachusetts in 1698, 39 were built in Boston, 38 in nearby Scituate, 25 in Salem, and the remainder in other communities. These ships averaged 50 tons. It should be noted that while shipbuilding was carried on in a number of places at this time, ownership of the vessels was concentrated almost exclusively in Boston whose residents owned 80% of Massachusetts tonnage.[11]

It would be another 75 years or so before Duxbury joined this industry in a significant way but the tradition was established early on with 19 vessels built between 1703 and 1713, all of them purchased by Boston owners. An average of two vessels were launched each year in Duxbury during this era. The typical vessel, at 35 tons, was a small sloop at best.

John Weston's house on Surplus Street, built c. 1730.

If family tradition is correct, John Weston built several of these early Duxbury vessels. His endeavors were an important factor contributing to the success of his descendants in the late 18th and early 19th centuries. Son Eliphas and grandson Ezra I would be born with shipbuilding in their blood, trained in the trade from an early age. Although John's work cannot be considered the beginning of the Weston enterprise, his era was a key prelude to it.

Around 1697, John married Deborah Delano. They had seven children, the youngest of whom,

Eliphas Weston, learned the shipwright's trade. In 1730, John Weston moved from his farm in the Nook to a new house that still stands on present-day Surplus Street. Several of his sons were still part of his household at the time. Eliphas Weston lived in the small Cape Cod style house until he came of age and married.[12]

John Weston passed away in his sleep in 1736 at age 75. According to his family, he died "of a nightmare."[13]

Eliphas Weston

About 1738, Eliphas Weston, shipwright and sometime fisherman, married Priscilla Peterson. She was a descendant of Pilgrim George Soule who had been granted most of the peninsula known as Powder Point. The Point extends a mile eastward from the Duxbury mainland. During Eliphas Weston's time it was bisected lengthwise by a cart path which would one day become Powder Point Avenue. Priscilla's father, Isaac Peterson, owned most of the Point on the south side of the cart path. His house, now gone, stood near the present-day corner of King Caesar and Weston Roads.[14]

Powder Point would thereafter be known as the domain of the Weston family. With a commanding view, broad frontage on Duxbury Bay, and proximity to the sheltered area of the Bluefish River, the location was ideal for the seat of a shipbuilding industry. Eliphas acquired his property partly through dowry and partly by purchase. He built a substantial house just west of his father-in-law's, the first of a row of three generations of Weston houses that would line the southern shore of Powder Point one day.

At this time, Massachusetts was enjoying a period of peace, prosperity, and unprecedented expansion. From 1713 to 1743, between wars with France, New England settlers spread west to the Berkshires and east along the Bay of Fundy. Fifty new towns were incorporated in Massachusetts. Countless new mills, shipyards, and iron forges were established. Duxbury saw the same expansion in microcosm. In 1712, the community saw fit to divide the common lands — the greater, unsettled part of the town west of present-day Tremont Street. Expanding west, Duxburyites carved out new farms and built mills on the tiny woodland brooks.[15]

And on the shore of Powder Point in 1738, Eliphas Weston commenced boatbuilding in a small yard directly in front of his house. He had an ample workforce in his eight sons, including Ezra Weston I.

On March 18, 1762, Eliphas Weston climbed into a small boat with his 14-year-old son Joshua. They were bound across the bay to Duxbury Beach to collect timber for the boatyard. George Cushman, who lived on the end of

South - Front of "John Brewster" house as it now stands 1855. & East end.

Powder Point, saw them go. Once there, they cut the cedar and loaded it into the craft, more heavily than was prudent. As they headed back for Powder Point, a strong wind blew up and it began to snow. The water quickly grew rough and filled the low-riding boat. Father and son drowned in the bay, within sight of their home, but for the snow. Joshua's body was found the next day. Eliphas's was found a month and a half later at Eagles Nest Creek, about three miles from where his boat went down.

Eliphas Weston house, built 1738, was located at the present-day corner of Weston and King Caesar Roads. Both the house and shipyard out front were inherited by Eliphas' eldest son, shipwright Warren Weston. The house was torn down in 1863.

This tragedy marked the beginning of a dangerous relationship between Eliphas Weston's family and the sea. Of his eight sons, four drowned. On November 17, 1766, Daniel Weston, master of a vessel bound for Bristol, Maine, perished when his ship went down off Duxbury Beach. Younger brother Timothy commanded a privateer during the Revolution, and he drowned when his vessel went down in the Bay of Fundy about 1780. After the Revolution, Eliphas, Jr.'s vessel foundered en route to Boston from Baltimore. The entire crew was lost.[16]

All of Eliphas Weston's remaining sons were involved in maritime trades, except perhaps Simeon, the youngest, about whom there are no evident records. Warren Weston, the eldest son, lived on in his father's house, building in his father's small shipyard. For the most part, Warren was a builder, not an owner of vessels.

Arunah Weston, who had built a house on the north side of the Bluefish River (where Powder Point Avenue today runs), decided in 1785 to remove to Bristol, Maine. He dismantled his house, loaded it on a schooner, and re-assembled it in Bristol. There, Arunah became a supplier of timber, a useful contact for his brothers in Duxbury.[17]

Ezra Weston I was 19 when his father drowned. Unlike his brothers who went to sea as captains, Ezra I chose to remain in Duxbury, carrying on his father's traditions as a shipwright. And unlike his older brother Warren, who also built vessels, Ezra I set his sights on a broad scheme that included ownership and operation of a large fleet. He clearly possessed a driving ambition unlike any in his family.

CHAPTER TWO
Father

The tide was in and it was time to sail. Captain Wadsworth paced the deck of his schooner, muttering curses as he watched vessels pulling away from the wharves on Boston's waterfront. Time to sail and their most important passenger was still not on board. From time to time King Caesar boarded one of his packets in Duxbury and went up to Boston to conduct business, returning later in the same day with his schooner.

Wadsworth checked his watch more than a few times. In all likelihood Weston was in some dark counting house in Dock Square, deeply engaged in a discussion of the value of freights in various ports. To wait much longer would mean missing the tide and possibly delaying their departure until the following morning.

Finally, Wadsworth grabbed a paper and pen and scribbled a message. He hollered for his first mate and thrust the paper at him. Bring this to the Town Crier, he said.

The mate, sensing that the message would result in no good, protested.

It's an order, Wadsworth told him. The mate had no choice.

The mate took the message and disembarked from the schooner. Surely this would lead to a row between King Caesar and the Captain, with the mate caught in the middle. He made his way up the wharf and was relieved to see Weston striding towards him.

As Weston boarded the schooner, the mate glanced at the note. It read:

> Mr. Crier, please to cry,
> A man which hath a light blue eye;
> A scarlet coat, a proper teaser,
> and is known by the name of "Old King Caesar."

He pocketed the message, greatly relieved that he would not be the one responsible for stirring the wrath of Old King Caesar.[1]

In order to understand fully the successes of the Weston enterprise, it is necessary to start at the beginning and to examine the accomplishments of the first Ezra Weston. Ezra I (1743-1822) was a man of remarkable vision and energy who built a sizeable fleet and had the courage to operate it during a dangerous era in maritime history. His most extraordinary innovation, however, and the one from which his son would benefit the most, was the foresight he showed in diversifying the activities of the firm, delving into many of the subsidiary industries related to shipbuilding. Eventually, this allowed Weston to build vessels without depending on suppliers of cordage, canvas, and other provisions.

And, of great significance to Duxbury's folklore, it was Ezra I's boldness and dynamic influence on the community that earned him the name "King Caesar," a title passed to his son.

The Foundation

The man who would one day be known by a regal title started out with a single sloop, the *Dolphin*, launched in 1764. Ezra I was 21 when he built the vessel, probably with help from his older brother, Warren.

There were seven Weston brothers left after Joshua's drowning during that fateful outing with their father Eliphas. All of them would be involved in maritime activities to some extent, as skippers, shipwrights, or merchants. They did not form a single Weston family business, however. Each operated independently, although they did take advantage of numerous opportunities to collaborate, invest together in vessel ownership, and otherwise assist each other.

Ezra I set his objectives higher than his brothers. Not content to be merely a shipwright like Warren, or a captain like Daniel and Timothy, or a supplier of timber like Arunah, Ezra I was determined to be all of the above and more.

Bills from various workmen indicate that Ezra I ran a busy shipyard in the late 1760s. Exactly where his shipyard was located at this time is unclear. He may have built directly in front of his house adjacent to his father Eliphas's shipyard on Powder point. At this early stage, he presided over the yard personally as the master carpenter, laying out the joinery of the vessels and supervising all aspects of the work. The timber for the *Dolphin*, indeed for nearly all his vessels, was brought in from Maine—in the *Dolphin*'s case from Broadbay, now the vicinity of Waldoboro.

Procuring good timber and paying men to haul it from the Maine forests and to measure it on the wharves was a complicated business. Ezra I frequently relied on his brother Arunah in Bristol, Maine to get this done. A letter requesting (or perhaps ordering) his brother's assistance also sheds some light on the frenetic pace of Ezra I's activity as a shipwright during his early career. Although there is an obvious quid pro quo involved here, it is clear that Ezra I, the older brother, is in charge.

Duxborough, July 22, 1771

Arunah Weston, Bristol

Loving Brother,

Hoping these lines will find you well as they leave me and all. Mother is as well as can be expected….I did not understand that you intended [for me] to build your vessel this winter. But Zeb Weston and I are all about building. I shall not build for him at all and I shall depend on building yours this winter. So go on to get your staff as fast as you please. I like very well that you should have the plank that Mr. Eaton got for me to build your vessel with…I shall want my spars in 4 or 5 weeks at the Fords and don't fail to have these ready for me when I send for them. Get something to load the vessel with. What vessel I send now, I don't know for as I am with Zeb Weston about building. But I shall be about freighting but some vessel I shall send and we will do the best we can about it. Write to me your first opportunity concerning your affairs. For what will turn up I don't know, but we will plan business as well as we can. So no more.

But I remain your loving brother

Ezra Weston[2]

The creative spelling on this pocket watch apparently did not greatly trouble Ezra Weston I, to whom it belonged.

By 1771, Weston had constructed at least five vessels in Duxbury on his own account—two sloops and three schooners. He retained at least partial ownership of this little fleet, and employed them in modest coastal trading and a bit of fishing. In at least one instance, he chartered out one of his sloops, the *Dolphin*, a ten-year-old vessel at the time in 1774, for a whaling voyage to be organized by a Colonel Erving of Boston.[3]

Weston also served as a carpenter in the shipyards of other merchants and builders in a variety of locations at this time. His bills

The Cottage

On April 20, 1767, Ezra Weston I married Sylvia Church.
Sometime before that, probably in 1766, he set about the
construction of his new house on Powder Point. Here,
on May 13, 1768, his first child, Sylvia Church Weston,
was born. Weston's wife died only 18 days later, undoubtedly
due to complications related to childbirth. Weston married
his second wife, Salumith Wadsworth, in 1770.
She bore him a son, Ezra Weston II, on November 30, 1772.
Five out of six of Ezra II's own children would also be born here,
before he built his mansion (now known as the King Caesar House).
The gambrel-roofed Ezra I house (later known as The Cottage)
was occupied after his death by a McLaughlin, superintendent
of the Weston farm. It burned in 1886 and was reconstructed,
larger than the original but
similar in appearance, by
Frederick Knapp in 1887.

Ezra Weston I house c.1865.

*Salumith Wadsworth (1742-1815), second wife of
Ezra Weston I and mother of Ezra Weston II.
Portrait by Rufus Hathaway c. 1793.*

Photograph courtesy of Abby Aldrich Rockefeller Folk Art Museum,
Colonial Williamsburg Foundation, Williamsburg, VA.

to his employers specify a broad range of services rendered, indicating that Weston was skilled in many of the crafts related to shipbuilding.

Of particular interest is his association with Marshfield shipbuilder Josiah Barker. In 1770, Weston spent March and April working on six of Barker's sloops, three of his schooners, and two of his brigs. He made new masts, caulked, and finished decks. The North River, forming the boundary between the towns of Scituate and Marshfield just north of Duxbury, had been a major center of shipbuilding since the 17th century. It is significant that Weston worked with merchants on the North River, particularly Barker, whose achievements must have made a strong impression on the young shipwright.

Weston also forged relationships with Boston merchants at this time. His success in doing so was an important factor in the growth of his activities. A mercantile venture based in Duxbury, a remote and nearly impoverished community before the Revolution, would require strong ties to Boston whence came all manner of provisions and supplies.

In the early part of his career, Weston was especially close to Captain Mungo Mackay (1740-1800). Mackay was a sea captain from Scotland and an up-and-coming merchant in pre-Revolutionary Boston. From him Weston obtained most of the provisions for his vessels between 1770 and 1774, particularly flour, sugar, molasses, and rum. Weston accrued a considerable balance on his account with Mackay, £295, which he paid off by building a 102 ton schooner and delivering it to Mackay on March 25, 1774.[4]

Weston's employment as a shipwright took him far beyond Massachusetts and Maine. A business associate formerly from Duxbury (who unfortunately goes unnamed) requested that Weston come to Nixontown, North Carolina to build a schooner for him. This represented a considerable amount of trouble and expense on the part of the employer, which says a great deal about Weston's skill. Ezra I reported his progress in a letter to his brother Warren, who minded his affairs while he was away.

> *Nixentown*
>
> *Loving brother,*
>
> *Worked on the Industry for she proved very lucky…I have got the biggest part of my frame cut and do expect to go to work in the yard next week. It is a very clever place to build and a very good cook to cook for us. My owner is in much better credit in this country then he was in Duxborough. He has enough estate to pay for two such vessels and very plenty. I have nothing more remarkable to write you about my business here. Pray don't fail to send and right to me concerning your welfare and what success you have and whether you meet with any difficulty about my business. Don't fail to*

embrace the first opportunity to let me hear from you and how all friends are.
Let Waterman's and Sprague's friends know that we are arrived and are
very hearty. So no more at present but remember me to mother and to all
known friends.

So I remain your loving brother,

Ezra Weston[5]

In 1773, Weston took on an apprentice, Amos Sampson of Duxbury, who was
indentured to him for the next four years to learn the trade of shipwright.
The story had come full circle for the Weston family. Edmund Weston had arrived
in Duxbury in 1635 as an indentured servant. And now his great-grandson,
Ezra I, was master of an indentured apprentice. The fact that an apprentice bound
himself to Weston indicates that Weston had mastered his trade as a shipwright
and was widely held in high esteem. He had built and refitted dozens of vessels
across Massachusetts as well as in Maine and North Carolina. He owned a small
fleet and carried out trade with merchants in Boston and beyond. The Weston
enterprise was poised for dramatic expansion.[6]

There would, however, be an impediment to Ezra Weston's plans.

Revolution

As Ezra Weston I was preparing to build his house on Powder Point in
1766, Duxbury was celebrating a triumph over the British Crown.
That year saw the repeal of the despised Stamp Act, a tax imposed on the
colonists by the British authorities in an effort to defray the costs incurred during
the French and Indian War (1754-1763). Opposition to the Stamp Act in the
colonies was fierce. Protests took a variety of forms, from the lofty resolutions of a
Congress formed by the colonies to address the crisis, to the tarring and feathering
of stamp commissioners.

There were no Stamp riots in Duxbury. However, citizens showed their delight
with the repeal of the act during a massive meeting on Captain's Hill. Once part
of the farm of Myles Standish, the hill was a powerful symbol to the town's
inhabitants. Six cannons were hauled to the summit on that March day of 1766.
Effigies of Lords Grenville and Bute were hanged on makeshift gallows, then
burned for good measure. Reflecting the mood of the occasion, no solemn orator
was chosen. Instead, a colorful character known as Joe Russell was appointed to
ridicule the "Lords" as they burned, much to the uproarious amusement of the

crowd. As the flames consumed the ropes and the effigies fell to the ground, Joe whooped, "There, I thought your station was below! I didn't think it was above. If ye'd been now an honest old ditcher as I am, ye'd never come to this!"[7]

Of course, the Stamp Act was not the end of the Crown's attempts to force the colonies into submission. Other well-known taxation measures would follow, and further resistance from Boston in particular would lead to the military occupation of that port in 1769.

Like most communities in Massachusetts, Duxbury watched the escalation of hostilities in Boston with anxiety and ambivalence. When put to the question, however, Duxbury showed its revolutionary leanings. The question came in the form of a pamphlet from the Town of Boston in 1773 asking Duxbury's support in opposing "the wrongful subversion of rights in the Provinces." A committee was appointed to respond to the Bostonians. The reply was drafted largely by George Partridge, Duxbury's Representative to the General Court and a future Massachusetts Representative to the Continental and United States Congresses. Partridge wrote,

Hon. George Partridge (1740-1828). The portrait is a copy of the original by Rufus Hathaway c. 1795. Duxbury's voice in the Provincial Court during the Revolution, Partridge was later a representative to the Continental and United States Congresses.

We inhabit the very spot of soil cultivated by some of the first comers to New England, and though we pretend not that we inherit their virtues, yet hope we possess at least some remains of that Christian and heroic virtue and manly sense of liberty…. We glory in a legal, loyal subjection to our sovereign; but when we see the right to dispose of our property claimed and actually exercised by a legislature a thousand leagues off, and in which we have no voice, and ships and troops poured in upon us to support the growing, or rather overgrown power of crown officers…we esteem it a virtue and a duty…to oppose tyranny in all forms…[8]

Duxbury's opposition to tyranny would be stirred further by the dramatic events of January 1775. Many loyalists in the adjacent town of Marshfield feared for their safety amidst so many patriots, so they petitioned General Gage in Boston for a detachment of the King's Troops to be stationed in their town. Urged by Nathaniel Ray Thomas, Marshfield's leading merchant and a Tory, Gage sent a company of 100 men under the command of Captain Nesbit Balfour from the 4th Regiment of Foot, known as the Queen's Guards. They brought with them two artillery pieces and 300 muskets to be used by the gentlemen of Marshfield against the rebels.

On January 23, 1775 the redcoats landed at the North River and marched through Marshfield to the estate of Nathaniel Ray Thomas. There they set up barracks, presenting a formidable force. Gage, pleased that someone in Massachusetts had, for a change, asked for his help, wrote to the citizens of Marshfield, "I feel great satisfaction in having contributed to the safety and protection of a people so eminent for their Loyalty to their King."[9]

Citizens throughout Plymouth County were outraged at the presence of so many redcoats nearby. The soldiers frequented Duxbury, many of them visiting the Old Ordinary on today's Tremont Street, not far from the Marshfield line. The troops were highly disciplined, however. On one occasion they did alarm Duxbury citizens by gathering outside the Meeting House, peering in the windows at the service that was taking place there. Although the soldiers did little to disrupt local affairs, many residents across the county knew that an eruption would inevitably take place.

Nathaniel Ray Thomas (1731-1787), merchant and gentleman farmer of Marshfield, played host to a garrison of 100 British soldiers in the winter of 1775. His farm (now known as the Daniel Webster estate) was the site of a tense standoff on April 21, 1775 between a British company and a battalion of colonial militia.

In the afternoon of April 19, 1775 news of the battles at Lexington and Concord spread across Duxbury. When Ezra Weston I received the word, he took his musket and joined the Duxbury minutemen who were forming up in the town. He was a private in the Duxbury company commanded by Captain Benjamin Wadsworth. His brother Warren was a sergeant. That evening, the Duxbury companies were joined by those from Kingston and Plymouth. They spent an uneasy night awaiting orders to march on Marshfield to confront Balfour's redcoats.

On the morning of April 20, Plymouth's Colonel Theophilus Cotton, the ranking officer commanding the minutemen gathering from across the county, held a council of war at the John Alden House, still standing, then the home of Lt. Colonel Briggs Alden. There is no record of the officers' discussion. But there was frustration in the ranks at the delay.

A day slipped by, and another night. Finally on the morning of the 21st, around 7 a.m., Cotton marched his regiment to Marshfield and took up a position around Anthony Thomas's farm, about a mile from the British garrison. This movement roused many of the crews of local fishing vessels who, eager for a fight, followed along. At noon, Cotton had about 500 men to Balfour's 100. While Cotton and Alden again held a conference, new companies arrived from Rochester and Plympton.

But Cotton did not attack. Around 3 p.m., the commander of the Kingston company, Captain Peleg Wadsworth, grew so impatient that, without orders, he advanced his company to within firing range of the British position.

Two British sloops appeared off Brant Rock: Captain Balfour had arranged his escape. He immediately began to load his troops on boats and, conveying them down the Cut River, boarded them on the sloops. Balfour later reported that, if he had been attacked, he would have surrendered without firing a shot.[10]

Ezra Weston's enlistment lasted three days. It was not the last time he would respond to a call to arms.

On December 6, 1776 British General Henry Clinton captured Newport, Rhode Island with 6,000 soldiers. Fearing an invasion from the south, Massachusetts volunteer companies streamed toward Narragansett Bay. Ezra Weston I enlisted with Colonel Thomas Lothrop's regiment on December 10. After the occupation of Newport, it became apparent to the American troops that Clinton had no intention of leaving the city. Rather, he would use it as a base to harass American shipping. Lacking an adequate force to dislodge the British, the Americans grudgingly withdrew. Weston's company went home on Christmas Day.

Newport remained a threat. In 1777, Weston responded to another alarm from Rhode Island, serving 33 days with Colonel Theophilus Cotton's regiment. Again, there was no invasion. It may well be that Weston never saw a British soldier during his three enlistments; however his service was commendable and surely not without hardship.

The war brought Weston's business affairs to a standstill. His active service in the militia, his work as a member of town committees to procure supplies and food for Duxbury and Boston, and, most significantly, the threat of the British Navy offshore, made it impossible to maintain commercial activities.

There is no evidence to suggest that Weston employed his small fleet in privateering, as did many of his associates. Mungo Mackay, his primary business contact in Boston, busily sought privateer commissions from the Commonwealth for the masters of his vessels. Mackay's merchant fleet, now a private fleet of war, succeeded in capturing several British prizes. Nathaniel Winsor, a Duxbury shipbuilder who, like Weston, had constructed and owned several small vessels

before the Revolution, outfitted at least one of his schooners as a privateer. H.M.S. *Chatham* captured Winsor's privateer, the *Olive*, off Duxbury's shore. She was released, but her mainsail was taken. A schooner belonging to Elijah Sampson of Duxbury did not fare so well. She was captured and burned within view from Duxbury Beach.[11]

If his vessels weren't involved in privateering, Weston may have laid them up in Duxbury harbor to avoid such dangers. It is more likely, however, that he sold his pre-war fleet because the vessels are not mentioned in records after the war. While the whereabouts of the Weston fleet during the Revolution are unknown, one thing is clear: They weren't conducting trade. There are no Weston business records between 1776 and 1780.

Massachusetts merchants, except the most adventurous who were willing to risk running past the British fleet, suffered considerable losses from the slowdown in commerce. Historian Samuel Eliot Morison observed, "The fishing fleet was in shambles after the war, either captured or decaying after being laid up for seven years. This led to the worst depression in Massachusetts history.... About 125 vessels had been launched annually in Massachusetts before the war. In 1784 only 45 vessels left the ways."[12]

Defining this depression more specifically, historians Robert Albion, William Baker, and Benjamin Labaree point out that, "the 1780s brought only disappointment and ruin to many merchants of the older generation.... To take the place of older merchants … came a new generation. Rising largely from among the artisans, shipmasters and privateers…. the profits they had accrued during the war were not tied up in defaulted bonds or worn out vessels and wharves."[13]

Weston belonged to that younger generation of middle-class artisans poised to take the place of the old pre-Revolution aristocrats. He, and other Duxbury shipbuilders of the same station, bounced back remarkably quickly after the war. The "worst depression" observed by Morison had little effect on them. In April 1781, while American forces began the process of cornering British General Cornwallis in Virginia, Weston acquired partial ownership of his first new vessel in roughly ten years. It was the schooner *Albanus*, owned primarily by Robert Pope of the firm Pope & Geyer in Boston. By May she had made at least two fishing voyages showing that, in the months leading up to the surrender, the British fleet was no longer a danger off the coast of New England.

Weston lost no time in capitalizing on this new opportunity.

The Sacred Cod

Ezra Weston, sir, we have sent you 1 anchor, 1/2 barrel tar, rigging and sparyarn, 1 compass, 1 pump brake, six gallons West India rum and an old cable which will serve and when you get here we will supply you with a better cable. Hope to see the schooner here soon.

Robert Pope

Boston, April 16, 1781[14]

Ezra Weston I made his first foray back into the world of commerce after the Revolution as co-owner of the schooner *Albanus*. This vessel was either built or refitted by Weston, with material sent by co-owner Robert Pope of Boston, in the spring of 1781. After stopping in Boston to take on additional provisions, the vessel set out later in April for a fishing voyage.

Here began Weston's 15-year reliance on cod fishing. The cod had already achieved iconic status in Massachusetts. In the early 18th century, the "Sacred Cod," a five-foot carved fish, was hung over the assembly hall of the Massachusetts General Court, a reminder of the humble creature's impact on the prosperity of the colony. After the Revolution, with new fishing rights granted to the United States on the Grand Banks, the fishing industry grew even more important.

To enter this venture, Weston relied on alliances with Boston merchants for much needed credit, which enabled him to build and outfit new vessels. To some degree he continued to depend on his old friend Captain Mungo Mackay. However, Weston also established new relationships after the Revolution that would have a lasting impact on his affairs.

Robert Pope was the first. Weston's joint venture with the firm of Pope & Geyer lasted for roughly three years, and though the association may not have extended beyond their co-ownership of the *Albanus*, it was enough for Weston to generate much-needed cash. His share of the fish caught aboard the vessel first paid off his debts to Pope, then allowed him to begin the construction of a new fleet in Duxbury.

The second, and most significant, of Weston's Boston partners was Daniel Sargent. Born in Gloucester in 1731, Sargent was a merchant in that town and in Newburyport, interested in the fishing industry. He took up residence in Boston in 1778 and became one of its most distinguished businessmen. In a family history, Sargent was described as follows: "he possessed a strong mind, a great store of good common sense. His decisions were promptly made and firmly adhered to . . .

His own education had been such only as his native town afforded. He knew most things that a merchant ought to know, but…his information was entirely practical." Here, then, was a man very much like Weston, who had risen to the top echelon of his profession.[15]

Beginning in 1783 and lasting well into the 1790s, Sargent became Weston's primary supplier of provisions, equipment for vessels, and goods for Weston's store in Duxbury. Initially these were supplied on credit. Throughout the mid-1780s Weston's debt to Sargent ran about £500, roughly the value of a fishing schooner at the time—no small sum.

Ezra Weston I (1743-1822). Soon to be known as "King Caesar," Weston had his portrait painted around 1793 by Rufus Hathaway. The portrait shown here is a later copy of the Hathaway done by Oliver Stearns in 1840. This version is virtually identical to the original except for the significantly improved detail of the face. Weston's son Ezra II was still alive at the time it was painted and may have commissioned this portrait to replace the very primitive original. Alden B. Weston noted that it was a good likeness of his grandfather.

Sargent supplied nearly everything Weston needed to outfit his vessels: nails, cordage, sails, and other items. When it was time for the vessels to sail, they were provisioned with Sargent's coffee, pork, flour, and rum. Weston's fishermen were equipped with Sargent's fishing lines and hooks. When Weston's vessels returned to Boston from the Grand Banks, the catch was sold almost exclusively to Sargent and he paid Weston's crews.[16]

Weston regularly purchased from Sargent a large quantity of staple foodstuffs, indicating that he had probably begun operating a store in Duxbury by 1785. The goods delivered to Duxbury are the usual country store staples including flour, sugar, salt, and molasses. One luxury item stands out in the records, however. Weston, it appears, developed a taste for chocolate. His Duxbury customers must have done so, as well. In the late 1780s Weston brought to Duxbury hundreds of pounds of chocolate each year.

There can be no doubt that the scope of Sargent's business made a deep impression on Weston. Sargent, who was 11 years Weston's senior and managed large-scale commercial interests, must have served as an important role model for the up-and-coming shipwright from Duxbury.

With sources of support and connections to the Boston markets lined up, Weston commenced the construction of a significant fishing fleet. Modest profits from fishing voyages began to pay off in a real way by 1789 as Ezra I climbed above his debts to Boston merchants. It should be noted that one local activity, perhaps Weston's first venture into diversification, played a significant role in paying off his accounts. In 1789 Weston paid many of his bills with deliveries to Boston of large quantities of tar. It is not clear whether Weston was involved in the production of the material or if he acquired it from another source in Duxbury. Tar was a well-known product of the town, used in caulking vessels and making cordage. One of Duxbury's neighborhoods still bears the name Tarkiln.[17]

This particular enterprise helped make 1789 a most productive year for Weston, who added three vessels to his fleet. The *Phoenix* was built by Weston in Duxbury; the *Prissy* and the *Lark* may have been purchased in Boston. By the end of that year Weston had at least eight fishing vessels in operation.

The early 1790s saw a hiatus in his shipbuilding activities as Ezra I focused on the operation of the fleet. With each vessel making an average of four fishing trips per year (and each bringing in an average of £200 per trip), Weston's gross income from fishing alone can be conservatively estimated at £6,400 per year in the 1780s. To put this in context, the cost of purchasing a Duxbury schooner at that time was about £300-£600. Records of Weston's expenses, and the amounts paid out to co-owners of the vessels, are not as detailed. However, the picture is clear enough to indicate that his profit margin was considerable.[18]

The catches were primarily cod, along with some mackerel. Weston's skippers delivered the fish directly to Boston or brought it to Duxbury to be salted, then sold in Boston. Weston added to his property on Powder Point saltworks, fish flakes for drying fish, and a large fish storehouse. These were the first, in the 1780s, of many industrial buildings that E. Weston & Son would construct on their Powder Point estate.[19]

Many merchants involved in the cod fishery chose the profitable market of the French West Indies as an outlet for their catches. Weston tried this at least once in 1788. The first Weston vessel to trade in a foreign port was the schooner *Phoenix*, which sailed that year to Guadeloupe. She made £353 by selling her cargo of salted fish. However she also paid out about £130 in duties, fees, and other forms of palm-greasing to the French registrars, the harbormaster, translators, military officials from the fort at St. Eustacia, and the customs house. Other merchants could afford this customary hurdle of foreign trade; however, at this stage in his business, Weston seemed to have no stomach for it. Later catches were sold almost exclusively in Boston, mostly to Daniel Sargent.[20]

1796 through 1799 were banner years for Weston's fishing fleet, propelling the firm into a new era of prosperity. At this time Weston began selling to several Boston merchants, moving beyond his relationship with Daniel Sargent, delivering large quantities of fish, for which he was paid in cash. To John Gray in October 1796 he sold $2,992 worth. To Payson & Holbrook he delivered a shipment worth $3,928. The skipper of his schooner *Prissy* gave Weston an account of fish caught from 1795 to 1796 indicating an aggregate value of $41,426. This steady stream of income, unlike anything he had ever seen, enabled Weston to commence the construction of a new fleet of 9 vessels in the late 1790s.[21]

This successful endeavor stands in contrast to previous assessments of maritime activity in Plymouth County. Samuel Eliot Morison indicates that the South Shore during the Federal period was at a "standstill," quoting a visitor to the region during that era. "The whole region," observed Dr. Dwight, "wears remarkably the appearance of stillness and retirement; and the inhabitants seem to be separated, in a great measure, from all active intercourse with their country."[22]

Duxbury, Kingston, and Plymouth were just beginning their ascendancy in Massachusetts maritime affairs while North Shore merchants at this time were already managing large fleets engaged in the China Trade. However, Morison's observation fails to take into account growing ventures of men such as Weston who were well connected to the intercourse of Boston markets.

Weston was not alone. Justin Winsor, 19th-century historian of Duxbury, wrote that in 1786 Duxbury sent 64 fishing vessels to the Grand Banks. There is

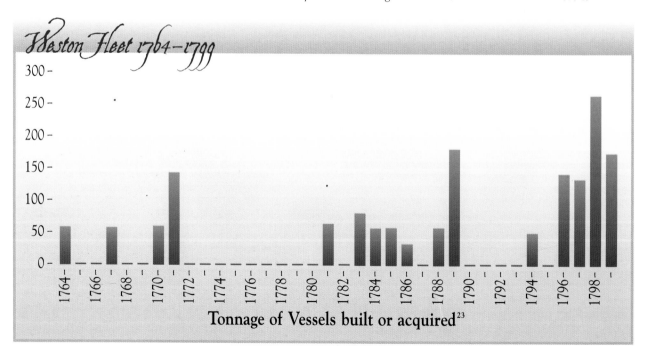

Weston Fleet 1764-1799

Tonnage of Vessels built or acquired[23]

no source provided for this data, and the statement should be taken cautiously. While Duxbury's fleet may not have been large, several shipbuilders were determined to take advantage of the new opportunities on the Grand Banks. Joshua and Nathaniel Winsor were among the first to lead the way with at least five vessels launched by 1786. Samuel Delano and Sylvanus Drew were others who followed. In Plymouth, the Jackson family (Charles, Daniel, Thomas, and William) had at least eight schooners in operation. Vessel registrations at the Plymouth Customs house indicate that at least 89 vessels were registered on the South Shore by 1799.[24]

By 1799, a pattern had emerged in the operation of Weston's fleet. Previously, he had depended on other merchants in Boston and Duxbury, as well as the vessels' skippers, to share the risks and expenses of ownership. In the late 1790s, Weston began to establish the practice of sole ownership, a distinguishing characteristic of the firm in the 19th century.

His financial independence established, thanks to the sacred cod, Weston sought involvement in other interests.

Vessels built 1780–1799 and registered in the Plymouth Customs District

Home Port	Number of Vessels Registered	Percentage of Total Registrations
Plymouth	37	42%
Duxbury	31	35%
Scituate	9	10%
Kingston	3	3%
Other	9	10%

Source: Ship Registers of the District of Plymouth, Massachusetts 1789-1908 (National Archives Project, 1939)[25]

The Ropewalk

Beyond shipbuilding and mercantile trade, ropemaking was the most significant activity in which Weston was involved. Given the importance and cost of good cordage, it is not surprising that Ezra I would consider the construction of his own ropewalk. In building the massive structure, Weston took his first and most important step in creating the independent and uniquely diversified operation for which he would one day be so well known. The Westons would soon be not just shipbuilders, but also one of the region's largest ropemakers, supplying cordage for nearly all the Duxbury shipyards.

In his early days as a shipbuilder, Ezra I acquired nearly all his cordage from John Gray & Son, the famous ropemakers of Boston. In the 1780s, when Weston was building small fishing sloops and schooners, the costs involved in acquiring cordage were not overly burdensome.

However, in 1796, with a sharp increase in the capital being brought in by the fishing fleet, Ezra I sought to broaden his activities and built his first square-rigged vessel, the brigantine *Rising Sun*. At 140 tons, she was twice as big as the typical schooners Weston had been building before. Her launch is one of several dramatic steps forward which mark 1796 as period of strong growth in Weston's empire. The choice of her name indicates Weston's awareness of his own ascendancy and good fortune in that year.

Rigging vessels of this sort was, of course, a larger proposition. The *Rising Sun's* bill for cordage in March 1796 from ropemaker John Winthrop of Boston was $2,238. It was a large sum, far exceeding any of Weston's expenses up to that date. While he may have considered making his own cordage before, after being hit with this bill, Weston immediately set about the task in earnest. Seven months later, he acquired his first supply of hemp (two tons from Eben Parsons of Boston), indicating that the ropewalk was probably ready for operation by that time.[26]

By 1799 the business was in full swing, as evidenced by the fact that an apprentice was indentured to Weston in that year to learn the art of ropemaking. David Darling, Jr., son of a Boston stevedore, served as an apprentice ropemaker for Ezra Weston for thirteen years until 1812. The next year Weston acquired another apprentice, Nathaniel Soule, who served a one-year term. Soule received training, board, and four dollars per month for his labor.[27]

Ropemaking required an extremely long building for laying out and spinning the cordage properly. Weston constructed his 700-foot-long ropewalk to the west of his house. In 1828, Ezra Weston II enlarged it to a length of 1,000 feet. The building ran from present-day King Caesar Road on the shore back to today's Powder Point Avenue.

Ezra I supervised the ropewalk personally for the first 20 years of its operation. Toward the end of his life he sought a new superintendent, employing Ephraim Bradford of Plymouth in 1819. Bradford had been the foreman of Salisbury Jackson's ropewalk in Plymouth. He would run the Weston ropewalk until it ceased operation in 1846.[28]

Bradford's son John, born in 1823, frequented the ropewalk even as a small boy. He remembered riding upon the horse, Honest Dick, who supplied power to the ropewalk's machinery by walking in a circle in the cellar of the headhouse. His labor earned the Weston family much profit, and not without gratitude. When Honest Dick died, four years after Ezra Weston II, Weston's sons had a monument constructed by the old ropewalk for this loyal animal to which they owed no small portion of their success.

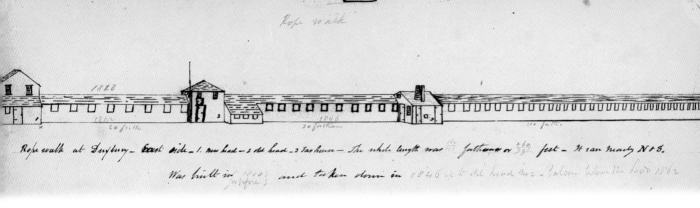

The Weston ropewalk, sketched c. 1840.

Later, John himself worked at a smaller wheel, supplying power for other types of cordage. Young men like John, who had just left school at age 16 or 17 and worked in the walk, occupied one of the lowest stations in Weston's enterprise. Bradford recalled his time in the ropewalk:

> The spinning of threads was done by hand. The men, usually six at a time, each with a bunch of hemp fastened about his waist, all moved with slow step backward. It required a good deal of patience for a man to spin an even thread, with no weak spots or bunches in it. It was monotonous work, the spinning and the boy turning the wheel that twisted the thread had a dull time of it, after the men had passed out of hearing he heard nothing but the rattle of his wheel for twenty minutes.[29]

The building was so long and dark that the spinners, moving slowly down its length, disappeared from sight. At their cue, the boys stopped turning the wheel and collected the newly spun threads, then brought out new bundles of hemp for the spinners. One thread might take the better part of an hour to spin. The larger stays (stout cables running from mast to mast) were made up of four strands of 200 threads each. Work began at sunrise and ended at sunset – a long, tedious day in the summertime.

In his reminiscences, John Bradford recorded the following verse:

> In that building long and low,
> With its windows all a-row,
> Like the port holes of a hulk,
> Human spiders spin and spin,
> Backward down their threads so thin
> Dropping, each a hempen bulk.

At the end an open door,

Square of sunshine on the floor,

Light the long and dusty lane,

And the whirling of a wheel,

Dull and drowsy make me feel,

All its spokes are in my brain.

Working the ropewalk was hard, but other Weston employees had it worse. From time to time, when a schooner tied up at the end of Weston's wharf, the boys were called out of the ropewalk to help the stevedores unload her. That, Bradford remembered, was back-breaking labor. Once, Weston's horse Jubah stepped on one of the boys. Captain Benjamin Smith, one of Weston's more distinguished master mariners, happened to be nearby and suggested applying the sailor's remedy of tobacco leaves soaked in rum to the injury.

Weston supplied complete rigging for all of Duxbury's major shipbuilders at one time or another. Rueben Drew, Joshua Winsor, and Levi Sampson are among those on record. For Weston's own shipyard, a controlled source of cordage was very important in keeping down costs. It was also a key source of profit.[30]

As of the turn of the 19th century, Weston's fleet was similar in scope to those of other Duxbury merchants. The fleet of Joshua Winsor was, in fact, larger. It was Weston's involvement in ancillary trades such as ropemaking that set him apart, helping to guarantee his eventual dominance over other Duxbury builders.

Honest Dick died in 1846, the same year the ropewalk ceased operation and was (except the head house near the water) dismantled. The Weston firm's shipbuilding activities were already at a standstill by that time. Perhaps the old horse's death was the last straw—a sign to be heeded. The Westons' ropemaking days were ended.

Ezra Weston I was master to at least four indentured servants who were to be trained either as shipwrights or ropemakers. A detail from the indenture of Nicholas McDonnell of Ireland shows the typical indentured seal at right.

Honest Dick, the Horse

A late 19th-century visitor to Duxbury walked on Powder Point.
Covered by tall grass, the field had once been the site of Ezra Weston's
huge ropewalk. Now its only feature was a curious monument.
The visitor recorded his bewilderment in a newspaper article:

> Standing out in the midfield at Powder
> Point, Duxbury, the other day, my eye
> rested upon a neat red brick column,
> surmounted by a big brown sphere.
> What kind of sundial is this? thought I.
>
> Judge my surprise upon approaching
> it to read this inscription.
>
> "We are all parts of one stupendous whole, Life is Nature,
> and God, the soul. Here lies buried Honest Dick. This noble horse
> served faithfully three generations. Born on Powder Point 1817,
> Here lived and died 1846."
>
> "That," quoth the native, "Why, that was King Caesar's horse."
>
> "And who was King Caesar?"
>
> He looked at me pityingly. "Ezra Weston," he said. "He owned
> the biggest part of the navigation of the United States once,
> nobody had so many ships afloat as he. That was why they
> christened him King Caesar. He set his life by that horse." [31]

Monument to Honest Dick, the horse, in its original location c.1890. Once the site of the Weston ropewalk, the field is now occupied by houses on the eastern side of Russell Road on Powder Point.

The monument was moved in the early 20th century to
property belonging to the Rural Society and still stands at the corner
of Powder Point Ave. and Bay Pond Road.

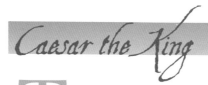

Caesar the King

The atmosphere of the Duxbury Town Meeting on January 17, 1803 was charged with animosity. Members of the meeting came ready for battle, and doubtless there were many who attended simply to watch the drama play out. For the past three years a storm had raged around a key topic. And it seemed this year the issue would be put to rest, one way or another.

The advocates of the plan in question were some of the leading men in town, shipbuilders whose new wealth commanded attention. Their schemes, however, seemed to hold little promise of benefit to the community as a whole.
The majority of the population felt that the advocates of the plan had only their own profit in mind.

Ezra Weston I, Seth Sprague, Joshua Winsor, and Samuel Delano, shipbuilders all, had made a bold proposal several years before. Prior to 1798, the shoreline of Duxbury was accessible only by crude cart paths running west to east at scattered intervals. This would not do for men who envisioned busy shipyards, stores, and wharves along the shore. For a shipbuilding industry to thrive, an avenue was needed that would connect the shipyards, running north and south along the water. This would allow easy transport of materials and convenient placement of workhouses, fish flakes, boarding houses, and all the necessities related to shipbuilding. Those with foresight might even have imagined the elegant merchant's homes and ship captain's houses that would one day spring up along such an avenue.

The plan had been realized, for the most part, in 1798 when work was begun on Washington Street, as it is known today. It did not happen easily. The advocates of the plan brought their case to court. They were opposed by the Town, which was loath to appropriate the necessary funds. The Court nonetheless sided with the shipbuilders and ordered the Town to begin construction. The road was laid out, branching northeast from the old Pilgrim-era path at the Nook (now Hall's Corner) and running two miles to the marshy shore of the Bluefish River. Here it came to a dead end. The shipbuilders had their avenue, and it would indeed provide the anticipated boost to their activities.

But the plan was not finished. In 1800, the year Washington Street was completed, the Bluefish River was a barrier to activities along the shore and an untapped resource. For Ezra Weston I, it was a particular nuisance. Living on Powder Point, separated from the rest of Duxbury by the Bluefish, he could view the new avenue from his side of the river, but he could not access it. To travel to his shipyard in the southern part of the town meant a long ride inland, around the headwaters of the small river. If the new road were simply extended across the mouth of the Bluefish River to Powder Point via a bridge, travelers and materials could be moved north and south along the entire waterfront.

Further, if a bridge were constructed near the river's mouth, a dam could be incorporated that would harness the river's power. In 1800 Duxbury's mills were far from the shipyards, some of them miles inland along woodland brooks. Here was an opportunity to create a forge and a gristmill right on the harbor's edge. Surely the new bridge and mill would become the center of a burgeoning industry with shipyards and stores springing up on both banks of the river.

The men who advanced this scheme showed remarkable vision, but their ingenuity was less than enthusiastically received. The bridge was proposed by Ezra Weston I at a Town Meeting in February of 1800. For a short time, it seemed as though he would have his way. The proposal was put to a vote and passed. Then, just before the meeting was ended, a motion was made to remove Seth Sprague as moderator. At 43, Sprague was poised to become one of the town's wealthiest merchants and shipbuilders. Well-respected despite his propensity for advocating unpopular causes, he would one day generate shockwaves in Duxbury by espousing the antislavery movement. Sprague had an interest in seeing the bridge project approved and perhaps he had steered the meeting too strongly in favor of Weston's proposal. The meeting voted that Samuel Loring, a Selectmen and a member of the group opposed to the shipbuilders' plan, should take over as moderator. Once this was done, a motion was made to reconsider the construction of the bridge. The motion passed and it was voted that no such bridge should be built.

The shipbuilders were forced to take another approach. As they had done with Washington Street, they brought their plea to court, this time obtaining an indictment against the Town for failing to complete the new road, including the bridge, as had been ordered by the court. This circumvention of the will of their community was, to say the least, audacious. Judah Alden was chosen to serve as the agent of the Town to answer the indictment in court. The "whole of the business" was left to Alden's discretion. He must have presented a compelling case in court. The Town was found not guilty on the indictment. There would be no punitive action against the Town for the delay, however, the Court held firm that the bridge must be built.[32]

Judah Alden, another of the town's leading men, was Duxbury's Representative to the Massachusetts General Court for much of the 1790s. He had served with distinction during the Revolutionary War, achieving the rank of Major in the 2nd Massachusetts Regiment. He was with the Continental Army at Valley Forge and, after the war, he fondly remembered his acquaintance with General Washington and the Marquis de Lafayette. Alden was proprietor of the town's first retail store, located in a house that still stands at the present-day corner of Alden and Tremont Streets. He depended on maritime trade but, as evidenced by his opposition to the Bluefish River Bridge scheme, apparently felt little allegiance to owners of the growing Duxbury fleets.

As agent for the Town, Alden did not stop at simply answering the indictment. Filing a new petition, he sought the court's support in discontinuing the majority of Washington Street, just completed, on the grounds that the road blocked, or would block if the shipbuilders had their way, a navigable river. If Alden had succeeded, the shipbuilders' efforts would not only have been stopped, but reversed. The shipbuilders had their way. Alden's petition was dismissed.[33]

Now, in 1803, the issue was brought before the Town Meeting again. The crowd was called to order. The voting men took their seats. In the gallery, young men, and probably a number of ladies as well, watched.

The decision on the first question, election of a moderator, was key. For the past decade, most Town Meetings had been moderated by Judah Alden. Lately, however, Seth Sprague had been chosen frequently. In fact, Sprague had also upset Alden in the elections of 1799 and taken his seat in the General Court, another symptom of the adversity between the two groups. Alden and Sprague stood on opposite ends of the issue at hand. The choice of moderator would have a

Revolutionary War hero Major Judah Alden (1750-1845) was a political opponent of Ezra Weston I and may have been responsible for immortalizing Weston's "King Caesar" nickname in less than complimentary fashion. Portrait by Cephas Thompson.
Courtesy of the Pilgrim Society, Plymouth, Mass.

powerful influence on the course of the meeting.

A vote was taken and Sprague was chosen as moderator. A coup for the shipbuilders.

The proposal was reviewed. Immediately, the expected arguments were raised. No one had a right to obstruct a navigable river.

It would be a drawbridge then, the advocates answered.

Then what of the cost, the opponents insisted. The estimated cost to the town for such a project was $3,000. This would mean an increased tax for all residents. Why should the town pay such an exorbitant amount for the benefit of a handful of shipbuilders and merchants?

The counter argument: a milldam would be a benefit to the whole community.

The debate must have proceeded for some time. Finally the question was called. Would the town construct a bridge over the Bluefish River? The vote was in the affirmative.

The opposition wasn't finished. A motion was made to reconsider the location of the bridge in a place other than where the court ordered. Whether this was a spiteful gesture to the court or to Weston, or both, is unclear. A bridge further up river would be shorter and cost less, which would be attractive to the opposition. It would also cause Weston to have to ride further out of his way, which also must have been attractive to the opposition. The motion passed.

Where then? A motion was made to build the bridge from the town landing to George Loring's property further upriver. This motion failed.

A motion was made to reconsider the vote to move the bridge. There must have been lengthy debate at this point because a vote was not taken on the question. Instead, it was voted to assemble a committee to develop a detailed plan for bridges in the two locations proposed. The meeting would reconvene in three weeks to review the plans and would then choose a location. The committee consisted of Ezra Weston I, Joshua Winsor, Samuel Delano, Seth Sprague, and William Loring.

Three weeks later, the committee had their designs. On a single sheet of paper, three feet long, were sketched elevations of two different bridges. The proposed bridge for the upriver site had no floodgate to allow vessels to pass (the river was barely navigable at the point proposed) and no flume for a mill. The bias of the committee was evident in the proposal. The upriver bridge would be

Seth Sprague (1760-1847) c. 1835.

cheaper but would offer no fringe benefits to the community. The bridge at the originally proposed location featured a 26-foot wide floodgate to allow for the passage of vessels (one foot wider than the town had requested) and would be surmounted by a small mill. The design was signed by Ezra Weston I.

Weston, probably enjoying an ironic jab at Town Meeting, titled the plans, "Harmony Bridge over the Bluefish River."

On February 3, 1803, the meeting reconvened to review the plans. The opposition, favoring the smaller bridge, argued that the cost of the larger bridge and milldam was far too excessive.

Seth Sprague, from the moderator's chair, agreed. It would indeed be an onerous cost to the town, he conceded. Perhaps if someone could be found who would conduct the work for half the amount, someone responsible whose work would be of the first quality, would the town then agree to proceed?

There was general agreement to his proposal, and probably a good deal of scoffing. Surely no one would agree to conduct the work for half of the estimated cost. A motion was made that the project proceed on the condition that the work cost

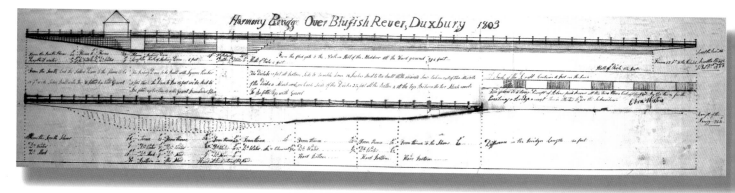

Plans executed by a town committee charged with designing the bridge over the Bluefish River in January of 1803. They are signed by Ezra Weston I. The plan at the top, with a wooden drawbridge and mill, was favored by Weston and ultimately chosen by Town Meeting.

no more than $1,500. The motion passed unanimously. It seemed Sprague had just doomed his own project to failure.

Immediately Joshua Winsor rose. He would accept the Town's offer, he said, and build the bridge for the stated amount.

The meeting was stunned.

The next day work began on the bridge. The opponents were so furious with the trickery, clearly plotted by the shipbuilders, that they tried to convene another meeting to reverse the decision. The construction progressed so quickly, however, that reconsideration was useless.

Although he was only one of several advocates, Ezra Weston I became the target of much of the opposition's frustration, perhaps because he stood to benefit the most from the new bridge. Shortly after the Town Meeting, an anonymous letter circulated about the town, lampooning the advocates and Weston in particular. The scheme was developed, according to the letter, simply so that Weston's property might be connected to "Sodom," the name given at the time to the growing village at the center of Washington Street (now the stretch of Washington from Snug Harbor to Surplus Street). Further, the author of the letter painted Weston as the culprit behind the shenanigans at Town Meeting. The letter read:

> And it came to pass in the days of Caesar, the King, that he commanded his servant Joshua, saying, get thee up a journey into the land of the Hanoverites, to Benjamin, the Scribe, and say unto him, I, Caesar, the King, have sent forth my decree, and commanded that the people in the land of Sodom shall no longer be separated from the Westonites, the Drewites, the Cushmanites, that dwell on the north side of the great river Bluefish. And also command Benjamin, the Scribe that he forth with make out a petition and convey it to the judges and magistrates of our land, commanding that they straightway direct the Sodomites, the Westonites, and all the Ites, within our borders, to build a bridge over the great river Bluefish. So the Judges and Magistrates, fearing Caesar, the King, and Joshua, his servant, commanded that the bridge

be built according to Caesar's decree. But it came to pass that there arose up certain of the tribes of Judah and Levi and of Samuel and of the Chandlerites, and other most learned in the law and showed unto the Judges and Magistrates, that Caesar, the King, had done wickedly, in commanding what was unlawful to be done, and so by the voice of the multitude the decree was set aside. And it came to pass that Caesar and the Sodomites wrought the minds of the people, and cast such delusions before their eyes, that they had fear before Caesar, the King and at length resolved to build the bridge, and connect Caesar's dominions to the land of Sodom. And now behold Caesar, the King, has erected an arch fifty cubits high on that bridge which the people, in their folly, have built, and set up an image over on top of the arch, and commanded all the people from the land of Sodom to the assemble on the fourth day of the seventh month, and bow their heads to the image which the King has set up. And behold the people assembled according to the King's decree, and did as he had commanded.[34]

Ezra Weston I would hereafter be known throughout Duxbury, and beyond, as "King Caesar." It was not uncommon during the period for local magnates to be known as "King." The letter's use of term indicates that the sobriquet had been applied to Weston before, hence the humor in the biblical spoof. But now the nickname had achieved legendary status. The title would be passed to Ezra's son who lived up to it well.

The author of the letter, and the man responsible for cementing King Caesar's larger-than-life persona in the minds of generations of Duxbury residents, cannot be positively identified. In his History of Duxbury, Justin Winsor offers two theories as to the identity of the author of the letter. One is Judah Alden, referenced in the letter by mention of the "tribes of Judah" who rose up in opposition against King Caesar. Given the years he spent opposing the project, it stands to reason that Alden might retort in such a fashion. Another possible author put forward by Winsor is Dr. Rufus Hathaway. As portraitist of nine members of the Weston family, Hathaway's criticism of Ezra Weston I would certainly be ironic. However, there is no indication as to possible motives for such animosity on the part of Hathaway.

The bridge was completed on July 3, 1803. Determined to prove to the town that this was a great accomplishment, the proponents of the bridge planned a celebration. They had the structure decorated with garlands. Carpenters constructed a wooden triumphal arch, which they set atop the bridge. This was crowned by a massive carved eagle which bore a motto from President Jefferson's inaugural address, "Peace, Friendship and Commerce with all Nations; Entangling Alliances with None."

The townspeople were invited to assemble on the 4th of July on the banks of the Bluefish. There, Duxbury's militia companies formed up, marched onto Harmony Bridge, and formed lines on both sides. Ladies in their finest dresses were escorted to the bridge and a large procession of citizens crossed under the arch. The shipbuilders had prepared a feast with long tables set out on a small hill (now called Fort Hill for the battery erected there during the War of 1812) overlooking the bridge. A jubilant Seth Sprague presided over the occasion.

The celebration was so splendid, it was said, that "many of the opposition received a check to their feelings of animosity, if they had any, and amid the scenes of mirth and rejoicings, many were the thanks expressed for the final completion of that much opposed, yet ably vindicated scheme."[35]

Ezra Weston I must have surveyed the festivities with distinct pride and satisfaction. Not only had the shipbuilders reshaped the waterfront and laid the foundation of an industry that would bring Duxbury much fame and prosperity, they had also demonstrated that their determination and influence could shape the town's policies. Weston had now achieved the same status in his own town that the patriarchs in Boston and Salem held in theirs. To be "King Caesar" meant not only wealth, but also power. King Caesar had found that, regardless of the opposition, he could have his way.

The next vessel he added to his fleet was his first fully rigged ship—at 300 tons a mighty large one for the period. He named her the *Julius Caesar*.

Harmony Bridge over the Bluefish River, painted c. 1880 by Professor Frank Howard. The original wooden bridge over the Bluefish River stood until replaced by the present stone one in 1883.
The building at right was a blacksmith shop and anchor forge. King Caesar's wharf is in the background. The present stone bridge is shown from the same vantage point.

CHAPTER THREE

E. Weston & Son

Partnership

On a hot July day in 1800, Ezra Weston II sat with quill in hand, prepared to take down a letter. His father, Ezra I was seething. In the history of the firm, nothing like this had ever happened.

Ezra II was 27. His father had taken him on as a partner two years before, at which time the firm was renamed E. Weston & Son. It would be so called until Ezra I's death in 1822. Ezra II had been acting as a clerk since he was 21, perhaps earlier. By 1800 much of the firm's correspondence and accounting was in Ezra II's hand.

There are no indications that Ezra II had any formal education or business training beyond basic country schooling. His handwriting and language were more refined than his father's rough scratchings but still coarse when compared with the flowery dispatches the firm received from their Boston associates. A sense of rural Yankee plainness pervades the Westons' writings and is evident in the manner in which they managed their affairs. Even after Ezra II became a prominent Boston merchant in his own right, these traits set him apart from the Boston elite. As described by his son Alden, Ezra II was, "A very energetic and active businessman. [He] was not fond of show, but rather retiring yet well acquainted with what was going on, of sound judgement." Ezra II's humble background and apparent disinterest in social or political affairs explains in part why the Westons, despite their astounding success, did not leave a more prominent mark on Boston's commercial history.[1]

Even without formal training, Ezra II showed a remarkable capacity for management. He was the first in four generations of Westons who did not start his career in a shipyard. He was intimately familiar with the shipwright's trade, of that there is no doubt. As a boy, he must have watched his father's fishing

*Ezra Weston II (1772-1842)
about the time of his wedding to
Jerusha Bradford in 1793.
A clerk at the time, in five years
Weston would become junior
partner in his father's firm.
Portrait by Rufus Hathaway.*

schooners being built. Later, even into his old age, Ezra II kept a hand in the shipyard's activities, giving his builders detailed specifications and ordering timber and other material with evident knowledge as to how they would be assembled. But there are no indications that Ezra II was ever a carpenter as his father had been.

The counting house was Ezra II's environment. Granted, he had done his fair share of time at sea, but this mainly in an administrative capacity. As early as 1793, at age 22, Ezra II was a supercargo in his father's employ. As historian Samuel Eliot Morison remarked, the position of supercargo, or business agent representing the owners onboard their vessels, "was often reserved for Harvard graduates, merchants' sons, and other young men of good family who had neither the taste nor the ruggedness for the rough and tumble of forecastle life." The position required an intimate knowledge of commercial practices in various ports.[2]

As the Weston fleet became increasingly involved in the coastal trade, Ezra II acted as his father's agent in North Carolina and elsewhere, securing freight. From an early age, Ezra II developed expertise in the art of selling and moving cargoes. Perhaps given Ezra II's youth, Ezra I felt it necessary to be clear with his master mariners as to his son's role in the firm:

> *Duxbury, December 11, 1793.*
> *Arthur Howland, sir, you being at present master of the sloop Jerusha, now in the harbor of Duxbury and presently to sail, our orders to you are that you embrace the first fair wind and weather that permits and proceed to the Pascotonck River in North Carolina. On your arrival there you will deliver your letter to Ezra Weston Junior, your consignee and join with him in trading your cargo on board, or deliver him your cargo to trade. If an opportunity presents to freight or charter the sloop, or any part of her, and you think it more profit of your owners than to proceed with their property, you will freight or charter to such port or ports as you and your consignee will think best…the said Ezra Weston Junior's orders shall be binding on you and your owners…You will keep a good command on board your vessel. You will let your owners hear from you by every opportunity, and for your commission on trade in Carolina five percent on sales and*

returns, divided between you and the said Ezra Weston junior…

So God send you a prosperous voyage and a safe return.

We are your friends and owners, Ezra Weston.[3]

Letter written by Ezra Weston I c. 1790.

By the time Ezra II became a partner (the first recording of "E. Weston & Son" being May 15, 1798), the firm was ready to move in a new direction—foreign trade.

It was a logical next step, however, after 1798, their affairs moved so deliberately in this direction that it seems Ezra II must have had a hand in setting the new course. Indeed, as a mid-19th-century newspaper observed, "Ezra Weston II possessed much more ability and capacity for business than did his paternal parent, without his sternness and rough exterior. The elder Ezra's success in accumulating wealth was in no small degree attributed to the tact and shrewdness of his son who was associated with him as a business partner nearly thirty years." This observation, made not long after Ezra II's death, has largely been forgotten as recent writers have primarily focused on Ezra I's role.[4]

On this July day in 1800, Ezra II, although skilled in tact, probably had a difficult time curbing his father's outrage. Ezra I began to dictate the letter, and Ezra II took it down.

This note, dated May 15, 1798, is the earliest document reflecting the change of the firm's name to E. Weston & Son.

The Weston enterprise had been relatively free of misfortune, natural or otherwise. Only four of approximately 110 vessels owned by the firm over the course of its long history were lost at sea. This is proof of the skill of the firm's master mariners and the Westons' acumen for choosing them.

The current embarrassing and unpleasant situation was an exception to this rule.

The sloop *Sophia* was built by Ezra Weston I in 1786. She was only 25 tons, the smallest vessel built by the firm. Despite her size, she was a profitable little sloop. For 14 years she made fishing voyages out to the Grand Banks with six or so fishermen on board, typically bringing in about £50 worth of fish per voyage.

There are 35 fishing voyages made by the *Sophia* on record between 1786 and 1796, making a total of £1,826, enough to pay for the vessel more than 12 times over. In 1795, Weston bought back half of the vessel from its former master and co-owner Barzillai Delano for £50. He then sold that half to a new co-owner for £100. The sloop was indeed a good investment.

Until 1800, that is, when the Westons engaged Reuben Young as skipper.

"Captain Young, sir," the letter began. "I have sent by Capt. Reed to you my account. I expect you will send back the vessel and pay the balance. As I have given Capt. Reed full power to act in my stead. I am very much astonished at your Rascally Conduct and wish to meet you in America so that I can deal with you according to your deeds. I expect Capt. Reed will in some measure as I have given him full power to act in my stead. E Weston & Son." [5]

Letter from E. Weston & Son to the rogue Captain Young, July 1800.

Young had taken the sloop out for a voyage, along with about $100 of supplies he had purchased from Weston on credit. He never came back. Weston somehow tracked down the whereabouts of the stolen sloop and the piratical skipper and engaged Captain William Reed of Provincetown as an attorney to secure the sloop's return.

There is no indication that Weston ever saw the sloop again..

French Spoliations

Seafaring has always been an occupation fraught with risk and danger. This was particularly so during the era in which the Westons commenced foreign trade. In 1798 a virtual state of war existed between France and the United States. It was known as the Quasi-War due to President John Adams's reluctance to seek a formal declaration in the politically heated atmosphere of the day. Revolutionary France, indignant at United States' recent treaty with Great Britain, unleashed its navy and privateers on American shipping. President Adams responded by encouraging the issuance of "letters of marque" from the Federal government, entitling American merchant vessels to arm and defend themselves against attacks by the French.[6]

In March of 1799, the ship *Mary*, owned by Boston merchants, sailed with Ezra II's brothers-in-law Gamaliel and Gershom Bradford acting as master and first mate. She was attacked by two French privateers. The ship had been issued a letter of marque and was well armed. The Bradfords fought off the privateers, safely making the harbor of Malaga, Spain. Unfortunately, the French followed them into the harbor and anchored near the American vessel. Gamaliel Bradford noted in his log, "The Frenchmen threaten very hard to watch us when we go out, but we shall be prepared for them and if they trouble us, we shall give them as good a dressing as they got before." The Bradfords teamed up with several other American merchantmen for safety, and the small squadron left Malaga at the same time and escaped unscathed.[7]

Bradford did not fare so well in a second encounter in July of 1800 while master of the ship *Industry*. Pursued by three French privateers, the American crew barely managed to drive off their attackers. In the fight, Gamaliel Bradford was hit by grapeshot just below the knee. The wound required the amputation of his leg. Upon arriving home, Bradford wrote, "I am once more in America my beloved country. After a long and disastrous voyage how pleasant it is to return. At present my joys are dampened by reflection on my unhappy state, but I desire to be resigned to it. I have not yet landed, but can see near where my friends reside."[8]

The Westons understood, then, the financial as well as personal risks they were undertaking in sending their vessels, crewed by friends and neighbors, on the high seas. A family memoir tells of a Weston vessel that was taken by the French during the Quasi-War, however the details of this encounter do not survive.[9]

This era of acute danger for American seafarers eased somewhat in the first decade of the 19th century after the Treaty of Mortefontaine in 1800. The seizures resumed in the years leading to the War of 1812 as the American merchantmen

The Letter-of-Marque
Industry of Boston engaged
by French privateers,
July 1800, depicted in a
20th century painting by
Leslie Wilcox. During the battle,
Capt. Gamaliel Bradford of
Duxbury was seriously injured,
but his crew managed to beat
back their assailants. As he was
taken below, Capt. Bradford
said to his crewmen, "Remain
calm, keep up a steady fire and
do not allow them to board."

Photo courtesy of
Mr. & Mrs. Gerald W. Kriegel.

once again found themselves in the middle of hostilities between Great Britain and France. In 1806 and 1807, both adversaries dealt out embargo orders, forbidding any of their allies to engage in trade with their rivals. Emperor Napoleon, angered by America's insistence on its right to trade with any nation, followed this with decrees ordering his navy to destroy any American vessels bound to or from ports in the hands of the English.

In December of 1811, Ezra I gave leave to Captain Jacob Smith to depart Boston as master of the brig Gershom. The brig had been named for Ezra II's eldest son who was six years old when she was launched in Duxbury. Her master carpenter was Joshua Magoun, the second of the Westons' builders noted in records. The appearance of the names of master carpenters indicates that by the turn of century, and probably earlier, Weston had relinquished control of the shipyard. Aged 63 when the Gershom was launched, Ezra I was a shipwright no longer, but now a merchant with broader concerns.

A proclamation issued by President Madison in 1810 stated that Napoleon had rescinded his threats against American shipping. The Westons could now send their fleet to Europe bolstered by a sense of relative safety. In 1811, their fleet consisted of roughly 20 vessels, half of which were larger brigs and ships involved in foreign trade. The Gershom, at 112 tons, was one of the smaller vessels.

On December 28, having gotten his cargo of flour, corn, and rice in order and cleared his papers through the customs office, Captain Jacob Smith ordered his crew to make sail. The brig made a course for Oporto, Portugal. They did not make their destination.

North of the Azores in the Atlantic, the *Gershom* crossed the path of a French naval squadron out of Nantes. Born down on by two frigates of 44 guns each and a brig of 16 guns, Captain Smith had little choice but to surrender. He and his crew were taken aboard one of the frigates while the French stripped the *Gershom* of sails, rigging, provisions, and cargo. The French then set the brig on fire.

Captain Gamaliel Bradford (1763-1824) c. 1795. A brother-in-law of Ezra Weston II, he survived two battles with French privateers.

As the Duxbury crew was forced below decks, they joined a group of prisoners from the ship *Asia* out of Philadelphia. The *Asia*, taken some days before, had also been stripped and burned. Captain Smith later testified, "We were treated in the most cruel manner on board the frigates; being allowed only three half pints water, and a piece of bread per day to each man, and a small piece of meat twice in a week."[10]

Ten days later, near the British West Indies, the squadron fell upon the brig *Thames* out of New Haven and captured her. "After some deliberation," according to Captain Smith, "the crews of the *Asia* and *Gershom* were put on board the *Thames*, with 100 gallons of water, 150 pounds bread, and half a barrel of flour, for the support of 37 persons, although they had great quantities of provisions on board the frigates."[11]

Before going over to the *Thames*, Captain Smith asked the captain of the French frigate why the *Thames* had not been burned.

She would have, replied the captain, if not for the fact that the French had so many prisoners aboard and needed to discharge them.

Frustrated, and known for a fiery temper, Captain Smith risked a parting shot at the French captain. Would he apologize, Smith demanded, for the illegal seizure of the *Gershom*?

The French captain flatly stated he had been acting under orders. He was authorized by the Emperor to burn, sink, and destroy all American vessels bound to or from any of their enemies' ports.

But those decrees were repealed, Smith insisted.

They were not, the French captain replied. He gave the master of the *Asia* a letter to take to the French consul in Philadelphia stating that the vessels had been seized based on the Emperor's decrees.

The Americans were then released. They made a fast run to St. Barthélemy— a blessing given the shortage of provisions. There Captain Smith secured passage to Martha's Vineyard and returned to tell King Caesar the unfortunate news.[12]

The Westons petitioned the Federal government for reparations, claiming that the President's proclamation had given them a false sense of security. Massachusetts Senator James Lloyd took up their petition and presented it in Congress on April 22, 1812. A merchant himself, he was sympathetic to their predicament. The matter was referred to a committee, then, three days later, it was discharged and handed over to the Secretary of State.[13]

More than 20 years later, Ezra Weston II still sought his due from the government. In 1835, he noted with interest a newspaper notice of a meeting, sponsored by the Boston Marine Insurance Office, for "all persons in this city interested for claims for French spoliations…to take measure for presenting said claims to Congress at the ensuing session." He pinned the notice in his notebook. Apparently, the insurance company's efforts met with some success as Weston soon after received a check in the amount of $7,625 from, he noted, "the commissioners for the brig *Gershom*."[14]

Still not satisfied, and apparently claiming other damages (perhaps relating to the unnamed vessel captured during the Quasi-War), Weston continued to seek indemnification with no further success. Decades later, his youngest grandson would recall sitting on his father Gershom's verandah and being told how, despite having received damages from the French government, the Federal government had unjustly refused to distribute reparations to the aggrieved merchants.[15]

War of 1812

On a moonlight night in 1814, 42-year-old Ezra Weston II stood atop the hill where the town had celebrated the opening of the Harmony Bridge 11 years earlier. The words on the banner that had hung on the bridge that day bore particular irony now: "Peace, Friendship and Commerce with all Nations; Entangling Alliances with None." The hill was no longer a setting for a banquet, but now the site of a crude fort, thrown together to protect the town's fleet from

British barges. The battery was fully manned that night, all watching the shore carefully. Ezra II, although the junior partner of the town's leading merchant house, apparently had little interest in leading military affairs. He was one of the drag rope men assigned to cannon three.[16]

The beacon on Captain's Hill was ablaze, as were others along the bay. The men in the battery could hear the militia known as the "Sea Fencibles," some of whom were from towns far inland, marching outside the fort. Perhaps they noticed a detachment of 30 men, under Captain Seth Sprague, break away and head toward the shoreline to search for British marines. None were found.[17]

The alarm was a hoax, according to later rumors, started by the "row guard" from their boat out in the Bay. Patrolling back and forth between Plymouth Beach and Saquish, they allegedly wanted to see if anything would happen when they fired a signal. It all became something of a joke. However, even as they jested, inhabitants of the South Shore knew the danger was quite real.

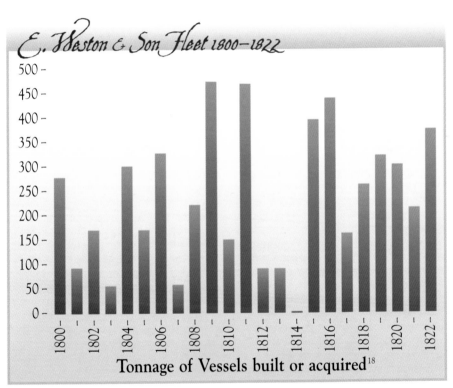

E. Weston & Son Fleet 1800–1822

Tonnage of Vessels built or acquired[18]

The War of 1812 caused the most dramatic slowdown in the Weston's shipbuilding activities since the Revolution. The three years leading up to the war had been the firm's most successful yet, even in the face of great hazards, with six new vessels built totaling 1,075 tons. At 337 tons, the ship *Camillus*, built by master carpenter James Southworth in 1811, was the largest yet commissioned by the firm. She was a big ship for her time, representing in a symbolic way the Westons' arrival as international merchants. The firm would not construct a larger vessel until the *Julian* was built in 1828.

Upon the declaration of war in 1812, the Westons' affairs hit a sharp downturn. They built no vessels in 1814. There had not been a year in the past 22 in which the Westons failed to add to their fleet.

The British men-of-war off the Massachusetts coast were to blame for the idleness in Duxbury shipyards and the stillness on its wharves. During the War of 1812, a squadron of the British Navy, including the *Spencer*, the *La Hogue*, and the *Leander*, patrolled Cape Cod and Massachusetts Bays, confiscating many American vessels in their search for privateers. Just 8 miles north of Duxbury, the town of Scituate's fishing fleet had been all but annihilated by the man-of-war *Bulwark*. Fear of a similar calamity kept Duxbury citizens vigilant in their watch for landings of British barges. Several of the town's larger vessels were hauled up into the Back River for safety and stripped of their upper masts so as to be less conspicuous.[19]

New England's opposition to the war, largely stemming from outrage at the harsh effects on the region's vital maritime trade, is well known. Adding to this complaint, New Englanders (Weston included) also harbored bitter memories of the plundering of their fleets by the French in the years leading up to the war. A war with obvious benefits to Emperor Napoleon waged by an ostensibly pro-French presidential administration was none too popular in the seafaring towns of Massachusetts.[20]

The Westons were no supporters of the war. Soon after the declaration, Ezra Weston I was a delegate to a meeting of Plymouth County towns in favor of peace. The meeting voted to circulate a petition, to be signed by like-minded individuals throughout the county, and to be printed in Boston newspapers.[21]

Similar sentiments motivated some members of Duxbury's Committee of Safety to propose sending a letter to the British naval officers offshore, professing the

View of Millbrook c. 1890, showing the mill once operated by the Weston firm from 1812 to about 1850.

1 m 11-4 lb. RIVETS,
Manufactured by
E. WESTON & SONS,
Duxbury, Mass.

1 m 11-4 lb. RIVETS,
Manufactured by
E. WESTON & SONS,
Duxbury, Mass.

1 m 11-4 lb. RIVETS,
Manufactured by
E. WESTON & SONS,
Duxbury, Mass.

A

Easterly or Back side Factory. & ... end
Waste Way *Outlet of pond ~ Brook*
DAM

Labels for Weston rivets, c. 1845. The mill, which originally produced sailcloth, was converted to a nail and tack factory; The mill of the Duxbury Manufacturing Company organized by the Westons, sketched c. 1840.

town's opposition to the war. Seth Sprague, once again a proponent of unpopular causes, had done much to ready the town for defense, including securing cannon for the fort, partly at his own expense. When Sprague petitioned the Board of War in Boston for more guns and ammunition, a member of the Board replied that the petition was pointless—the inhabitants of Duxbury would not know how to use the cannons if they got them. Sprague persisted and got his cannon.[22]

Deeming the Duxbury Committee of Safety's letter of neutrality proposal treasonable, Sprague loudly urged the rest of the committee to reject the idea. It was formally voted down, however some members of the committee nonetheless wrote a letter secretly and sent it to Captain George Collier of the H.M.S. *Leander*. Captain Collier's reply read, in part, " . . . Nothing but neutrality the most perfect will induce me to respect your fishing craft of the town itself . . . Do not allow your fishermen to assist [the war] directly or indirectly, as any deviation will be marked . . . "[23]

With their fleet and shipyard idle, the Westons looked to another outlet for their energies. In 1812, they established the Duxbury Manufacturing Company. On the Duck Hill River, not far from the homestead of their ancestor Edmund Weston, the Westons constructed Duxbury's only textile factory. Sixty feet long, the building adjoined a blacksmith shop. Launching thus into the production of sailcloth, the firm E. Weston & Son was now almost entirely self-sufficient, having the ability to control the costs of those raw materials most important to shipbuilding. The mill eventually included the production of wool and, later, was converted to a nail and tack factory.[24]

As soon as the war ended, the Westons re-commenced shipbuilding at the same pace as before, their capabilities apparently undiminished.

The Middle Fleet, 1800–1822

The middle period of the firm is characterized by the construction of larger "deep water" vessels, fully half of them brigs and ships. Business records from this era are few, therefore there is little detail available about the trade routes of this sizeable fleet. There are indications that, at this time, the Westons were most interested in southern European and Mediterranean ports in Portugal, Spain, and France.

The brig *Globe*, built at the very end of the period, frequented the port of Malaga, Spain. Her master was Jacob Smith, the same master who had been detained by the French in 1812. Having served the Westons faithfully as master of at least two other vessels during the 1810s, he was apparently undeterred by his experience with the French and had become one of the firm's key players. Although company records for the 1820s are incomplete, it appears Smith was master of the *Globe* for more than ten years. How furious he must have been when his successor ran the brig aground on rocks off Cohasset, Massachusetts. The brig was floated, but it was so badly damaged that Weston sold her immediately in Boston.[25]

The average vessel in the Westons' "middle fleet" was small, only 114 tons.

The private signal of the Weston Fleet, sketched by Alden B. Weston, manager of the firm's counting rooms, about 1840. Flown from the foremast to identify vessel ownership, this signal was used by the Westons by 1809. It was soon recognized around the world.

*A rare view of an early Weston vessel. Built in Duxbury in 1808, the 223-ton **Minerva** was only the second fully-rigged ship (three masts, square rigged) owned by the firm. Three times as big as their early coastal schooners, the **Minerva** represents the Weston firm's new success in overseas trade. Her bright colors are typical of merchant vessels around the turn of the 19th century. By the 1820s, austere black and white became more fashionable. This 1809 painting is the earliest image of a Weston vessel to show the red, white, and blue Weston flag, which came into use about that time. Watercolor by James W. Williams.* Photograph courtesy of the Peabody Essex Museum.

But there were many of them. Toward the end of the 1810s, the firm was managing as many as 20 vessels simultaneously.

It was during this period that the activities of the Weston firm surpassed the other merchant houses based on the South Shore. The table on the following page shows the number and tonnage of vessels registered in the Plymouth customs district by the top ten fleet owners in Plymouth County during the first quarter of the 19th century. It should be noted that several Weston vessels were registered in Boston and therefore these numbers do not indicate the full extent of his fleet. The same is probably true for the other merchants. Although incomplete, the sampling provides an adequate basis of comparison in order to determine the relative sizes of Plymouth County merchant fleets.

Vessels built 1800-1824 and registered in the District of Plymouth

Name	Home Port	Number of Vessels Registered	Tonnage of Vessels Registered	Percentage of Total Registered
Ezra Weston I and II	Duxbury	24	4,087	7%
Thomas Jackson and Sons	Plymouth	18	3,125	5%
Sylvanus Drew and Sons	Duxbury	14	2,909	5%
William Davis	Plymouth	14	2,075	4%
Joseph Bartlett	Plymouth	9	1,960	3%
Samuel A. Frazar	Duxbury	15	1,776	3%
Phineas and Seth Sprague	Duxbury	11	1,587	3%
Nathaniel Winsor, Sr. and Jr.	Duxbury	9	1,515	3%
David Kingman & Samuel Hicks	Hanover	4	1,408	2%
Barnabus Hedge, Sr. and Jr.	Plymouth	7	1,340	2%
Total		**125**	**21,782**	**37%**

Source: *Ship Registers of the District of Plymouth, Massachusetts 1789-1908* (National Archives Project, 1939)[26]

The ***Ezra & Daniel***, *built in Duxbury in 1805 and jointly owned by the Weston firm and Captain Daniel Hall of Duxbury, was typical of the small brigs of the Westons' "middle fleet." This is the earliest known portrait of a Weston vessel.*

Settlement

Ezra Weston I died on October 13, 1822 at age 79. During his lifetime Duxbury had been transformed from a humble farming community of roughly 900 to a town filled with flourishing shipyards and populated by 2,400. Duxbury's success and fine reputation for producing first-rate sailing vessels had been earned in large part by Ezra I's efforts. In the year he died, the firm of E. Weston & Son operated a ropewalk, a saltgrinding mill, several farms, a busy wharf with various storehouses, two blacksmith shops, a general store, and a textile mill. Since the launch of his first sloop in 1764, Ezra I had built or purchased at least 64 vessels.

He left no will. This led to controversy between his son Ezra Weston II, and his son-in-law Sylvanus Sampson (who had married Sylvia Church Weston about 1787). Sampson (1761-1848) was also a shipbuilder and merchant, albeit on a smaller scale than his father-in-law. He lived and maintained a busy store in a house on today's Standish Street with a nearby wharf at the mouth of Eagles Nest Creek.

As Sampson and Ezra II set about dividing the estate, a rift soon formed between them. The episode is significant not because of the disagreement. Both men were simply pursuing the best interests of their families. Rather, it is worthy of consideration because the issues that arose shed light on the scope of the firm and, more particularly, on a curious aspect of its operation.

The first step in dividing the estate, naturally, was to determine the assets and liabilities of the firm. Ezra Weston II could not, or would not, supply this information. A confounded Sampson wrote him shortly after Ezra I's death, "You wish a settlement. So do I. A full and fair account must first be made out before a settlement can be attained. This account must be furnished by you . . . If the books are in such a state as you say, you cannot furnish a true account from the books, I shall not object to settle by compromise. But then this compromise must be a just one . . ."[27]

It is impossible to determine whether Weston was being obstinate or he simply lacked the ability to furnish a proper statement. Probably, it was a combination of the two. The crux of Weston's difficulty was his claim, without documentation, that his father had turned over to him certain property to be his own, separate from the firm. Ezra II's elegant house, for instance, had been built on his father's land but was, he claimed, his personal property. However, the land had not been deeded to him. In addition to these vague areas of title there may have been real problems in record keeping. That the Westons had a natural genius for management in an international arena cannot be denied. However, their lack of formal business training is evident where the early records of the firm are concerned. The surviving records of the firm are unsystematic. This deficiency would be rectified shortly after the settlement when Ezra II appointed his son Alden B. Weston as his chief clerk around 1825. Alden's records would be meticulously detailed.

Arbitrators were brought in to evaluate the firm's assets. The process was difficult. At times, Sampson lost hope that an equitable solution could be achieved and contemplated quitting the effort. His son, Ezra Weston Sampson, urged him to keep at it, "Be not dispirited...Weston thinks to wear you out. Never! Give Weston as a final answer you will never leave the firm affairs to a referee. You cannot do a worse thing... You have bent the knee to Baal too long. It does no good to sit down in the chimney corner and complain of your vexations. Show yourself resolute." [28]

Mourning ring for Ezra Weston I, 1822. This ring, worn by his daughter Sylvia Church Weston Sampson, contains a small lock of the first King Caesar's hair.

As the issue dragged out for three years, Weston found himself in what must have been an uncomfortable and frustrating situation, sharing ownership of the firm with his brother-in-law who, heretofore, had had nothing to do with the firm's operations. As matters arose that required decisions, Weston was evidently bound to seek Sampson's input. The following letter from Weston to Sampson is an example:

March 25, 1823. Sir...It is necessary that Capt. Thomas should have some advice soon. I have no letter from him. Shall I direct him to proceed direct to Boston or take a freight from Baltimore for Europe if one should offer or to sell the schooner in Baltimore and if the latter, at what price? Should Capt. Thomas take a freight from Baltimore, the ownership in the schooner to continue the same as at present? Please write me your wishes on this thing.
Truly yours, E. Weston. [29]

An assessment was finally achieved. The net worth of the firm was shown to be roughly $116,000, equivalent to about $25,000,000 today based on the unskilled wage rate. The inventory on the next page provides a good indication of the scope of the firm. [30]

Items listed in Ezra Weston I estate settlement inventories

Amount of vessels	$44,000
Amount of cash in England and elsewhere	28,062
Amount of debts due to company	15,167
Stock	10,490
Ropewalk	4,100
12 shares in Duxbury Manufacturing company	3,600
New dwelling house [Ezra Weston II house]	3,200
Wharf and flats	2,300
Goods in different stores	1,940
Old dwelling house [Ezra Weston I house]	1,300
Lot of land to the Pump, 21 acres	1,095
Lewis Sampson farm in Duxbury	1,000
Stock of cordage in ropewalk	900
Barn with shed and land	850
First lot of land, 10 acres, adjoining ropewalk	850
Webb and Southworth lot	780
Large store and sail loft	650
Hay	600
Cattle	600
Second lot of land, 11 acres	576
One share of Jones River Manufacturing company	500
5 shares in Plymouth Bank	500
Ray Thomas wood lot Marshfield	468
Horse barn	400
Pilot boat	350
One company lot from Joseph Cushman adjoining Cedar Pond	323
Joyce house and land	300
Store on wharf	260
New store and counting room	250
Two fish stores on first lot	240
Due from Sylvanus Sampson	187
Store with counting room	175
Mackenzie house and land	150
Tar store	120
Old work house	110
Lot from John Nash	70
Wood lot by his ancestors, 3 acres	66
Fish flakes	40
Two horses	30
Two sleighs	30
Lot from Jonathan Peterson	30
Small lot, 95 rods	29
Sheep barn	25
Gravuering kettle set with brick	20
One shed at meeting house	18
Probable amount the company may owe	-10,600
	$116,151

Not quantified but mentioned in documents: 2 house lots in South Boston, shares in Boston's Long Wharf, 11 pigs, 12 oxen, 1 cow, 4 heifers, 1 bull, 1 horse, 1 colt, tomb in Duxbury, 5 gold watches[32]

Even after the matter was resolved, the bitterness lingered. A poignant note to Sampson, which is unsigned but appears to be from Ezra Weston II, sums up the conflicting emotions of the situation. "I have not the gift of tongues, or the advantage of an education, but may it please you I have a principle of honesty and justice, between man and man and between a brother and a sister and hope I shall always have fortitude good enough to retain those principles to the last."[33]

At age 53, Ezra II was now the sole owner of the firm E. Weston. Great changes and dramatic growth in the firm's activities were soon to come. Duxbury had a new King Caesar.

CHAPTER FOUR
The House

The house that Ezra Weston II could finally call his own was the centerpiece of an awe-inspiring estate on Powder Point. The property had undergone many changes since his grandfather Eliphas Weston first erected a house there in 1738. A peculiar blend of country manor and industrial complex, the estate had no clear division between home and workplace. Almost immediately, the King Caesar House held a certain aura for the community and would breed as many myths as the man.

Surrounded thus by the sounds of men working, machinery turning, barrels and bales being hoisted onto schooners, Ezra Weston II's wife, Jerusha Bradford Weston, set about keeping house. There is little documentation pertaining to the domestic life of the Weston family beyond the existing physical evidence in the house.

However, the surviving decorative elements suggest that Jerusha was a woman of refined tastes who strove to create a setting in the house and on the grounds fitting the stature of King Caesar.

The King Caesar House as it appears today, and as it appeared in a sketch c.1840.

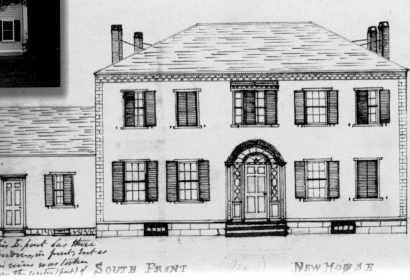

This S. front has three windows, in front, but as this view was taken from the center (front) of SOUTH FRONT   NEW HOUSE

An adolescent Gershom Bradford Weston, King Caesar's oldest son, lay sick in his boarding-house bed. The year was about 1815. Young Gershom was the first Weston to receive any schooling beyond the one-room schoolhouse. As a small lad, he had been privately tutored by the Reverends Norton of Weymouth and Morrill Allen of Pembroke. Now he was in the midst of a two-year spell at a Boston boarding school.

Gershom had come down with the measles. His boarding house landlady was less than attentive, but she did manage to get a message off to Mrs. Weston to tell her that her boy was sick. Jerusha Bradford Weston arrived in her son's room three days later, about as quickly as could be expected. Shocked to find that the room had not been darkened, she immediately drew the curtains, probably with some stern words to the landlady. Jerusha's arrival saved her son's sight, but some damage had already been done. Gershom suffered from weak eyes for the rest of his life, and he often needed to wear dark glasses as a result.[1]

Jerusha Bradford Weston (1770-1833) c. 1793. The portrait was painted by Rufus Hathaway about the time of her marriage to Ezra Weston II.

Photograph courtesy of
Abby Aldrich Rockefeller Folk Art Museum,
Colonial Williamsburg Foundation,
Williamsburg, VA.

Jerusha Bradford was born to Colonel Gamaliel and Sarah Bradford on January 30, 1770. She was almost two years older than Ezra Weston II. Colonel Bradford, having served in the French and Indian War, was a greatly respected man. A colonial magistrate before the outbreak of the Revolution, he found himself in a difficult position. Duxbury citizens, for the most part, favored the patriot cause. Bradford was one of the few in Duxbury who took a loyalist position being loath to spite the British Crown officials who had appointed him. This position soon became uncomfortable, however, and Bradford, along with fellow magistrate Briggs Alden, offered a public recantation of their position and an apology on September 14, 1774. Fully espousing the patriot cause, Bradford later became Colonel of the 14th Massachusetts Regiment in the Continental Army.[2]

The Colonel owned a large, 90-acre farm that straddled Tremont Street. It would one day be divided between three of his sons, Jerusha's brothers Gamaliel, Jr., Daniel, and Gershom. All three were successful master mariners. Two of them worked for Ezra Weston I—Daniel in charge of the brig *Rising Sun* in 1797, Weston's first square-rigged vessel, and Gershom as master of the schooner *Flora* in 1810. Two of the brothers built houses on their father's farm simultaneously in 1808.

*Rufus Hathaway portrait of
Maria Weston (1794-1804)
c. 1804. The first child of
Jerusha and Ezra Weston II,
Maria died at age 9.
Of six Weston children,
three did not survive childhood.*

Photograph courtesy of
Abby Aldrich Rockefeller Folk Art Museum,
Colonial Williamsburg Foundation,
Williamsburg, VA.

*Jerusha Weston's signature,
apparently the only
extant sample of her writing.*

The King Caesar House was constructed at the same time. The three houses exhibit certain identical features and details, primarily in the interior and exterior moulding, indicating that they may have been constructed by the same craftsmen.

The marriage of Ezra Weston II and Jerusha Bradford took place on June 2, 1793. To commemorate the occasion, Ezra I commissioned artist Rufus Hathaway, an itinerant painter from Taunton who would one day settle in Duxbury, to paint portraits of his son and daughter-in-law. Hathaway was not a trained artist. He painted in a rough, primitive style. The portraits were nonetheless a fine symbol of status. Very few in post-Revolutionary Duxbury could afford such an extravagance (the Winsors and Westons were the only Duxbury families who employed Hathaway). The portraits were probably a point of pride, but they provide only a vague impression of what the Westons actually looked like. Jerusha, about 23, is shown in a stylish silk gown, holding a small bouquet. Ezra II, about 21, sits with letter in hand, a quill next to him indicating the clerical nature of his duties.

Jerusha had to wait 16 years after her marriage for the construction of a house of her own. From 1793 until the completion of the King Caesar House in 1809, she resided in her father-in-law's house on Powder Point. With only Ezra I and his wife Salumith living there, there was room enough for the young couple and, eventually, their family, too.

Jerusha gave birth to five children in the old house. Three of them would be lost before the new house was built—Maria at age 9, Ezra III at age 8, and Jerusha at 19 months. The two daughters died within a month of each other, and so it has been suggested that a contagious illness was to blame. The surviving sons, Gershom Bradford Weston (born in 1799) and Alden Bradford Weston (born in 1805), were soon joined by Ezra Weston IV (the only child of Ezra II and Jerusha to be born in the King Caesar House) in 1809.

The three boys were raised by Jerusha on the Weston estate.[3]

Of Jerusha's life and personality, very little is known. It seems none of her letters have survived. The only scrap of her handwriting in evidence is her signature on a receipt. Her role in managing the Weston household and the complexities she undoubtedly experienced in being the wife of King Caesar must have been challenging. Unfortunately, this facet of the story cannot be explored in depth.

According to notes jotted by her son Alden for a family genealogy, Jerusha was

> *…lively and sociable. In youth she had red hair which changed to brown. Was good natured and obliged, was in fact such as a woman ought to be. Was fond of the society of young persons, was a good housekeeper, latter part of her life suffered much from sickness, liver complaint, was neighborly and charitable.*[4]

Her portrait by Rufus Hathaway, Alden added, was "not very good."

According to tradition, Jerusha was fond of flowers. One of the few shreds of idyllic ornamentation on the industrial property was a large, oval-shaped garden. It was inharmoniously situated on the west side of the house with the tarhouse and ropewalk as its backdrop. Jerusha took pains to have rare perennials imported from afar. One of these immigrants survived until the late 19th century, though the garden was long derelict by that time. The Knapp family discovered the curious flower when they occupied the estate in 1886. It was found to be a rare *iris reticulata*, probably brought to Mrs. Weston from the shores of Turkey.[5]

Sadly, one of the more carefully documented details of Jerusha's life is the prolonged illness leading to her death on October 11, 1833. She was cared for, in large part, by her niece Elizabeth Bradford, daughter of Jerusha's younger brother Gershom. The Bradford daughters (there were four) and the Weston sons were always close. Elizabeth wrote to her sisters, two of them in Ohio at the time, about their aunt's worsening condition. "I am sorry Aunt Jerusha is so sick," Lucia Bradford wrote back, "She must be very sorrowful, I should think. She always liked to go out so much."[6]

As to his emotions during the ordeal, King Caesar is silent, save one line. Wrapping up a letter to the master of the brig *Minerva* on September 6, 1833, King Caesar writes, "…You no doubt will be on the lookout for something [a cargo] for the ship. There is nothing a doing in Boston. My wife is very sick. Yours, E. Weston." Was this a perfunctory remark? Not so when considered in context. This line is the only mention, in all of Weston's business letters, of his personal life. It is significant that his wife's illness is even mentioned. A few months after Jerusha's death, Ezra II purchased a small black book for scribbling notations. Folded in the back is a small piece of embroidery, probably by Jerusha, which he carried with him for years.

Embargo

Surely Ezra II had the means to construct a new house shortly after his marriage if he had so desired. However, practicality was a defining theme in his life. His father's austere gambrel-roofed house was evidently sufficient.

King Caesar's parlor with one of Frederick Knapp's daughters wearing her grandmother's dress, c. 1910. The Knapp family owned the house from 1886 to 1937. The Knapps arranged photographs of their daughters in antique dresses to capture the look of the house during King Caesar's day.

And there were always ships to commission, perhaps a better use of capital than a new residence. Why then, would he suddenly order the building of a graceful manor after fifteen years of marriage?

There was an outbreak of house construction on the part of Duxbury merchants and master mariners in 1807 and 1808. Merchant Nathaniel Winsor, Jr. led the trend with a striking, three-story, stylish, Federal house in 1807. Looking as though it had been transplanted from Boston, the house was unlike anything that had been seen in Duxbury before. Three of Ezra II's brothers-in-law finished houses in 1808, including a handsome and architecturally unique house owned by Gamaliel Bradford. The road for which Ezra I and others had fought ten years before was now filling in with large dwellings.

Out on Powder Point, the King Caesar House was begun in 1808 and finished in 1809, toward the end of the building boom. Weston certainly did not initiate the trend. Perhaps, given the timing, Weston ordered the construction of a new home so as not to be outdone.

This increase in house construction is an indication of the success achieved by those in Duxbury who engaged in maritime affairs after the Revolution. Its timing is also related to forces at work far beyond Duxbury.

The ongoing conflicts between Great Britain and France in the first decade of the 19th century have already been noted. Seeking to protect America's maritime interests from further damage inflicted by onerous European trade restrictions and threatening imperial decrees, President Thomas Jefferson in 1807 declared a trade embargo. American merchant vessels were forbidden to conduct any foreign trade.

Etched compass rose in front of the King Caesar House. In Duxbury it was said that the points of the compass stood for "Ezra Weston's New Ship."

Fishing vessels could only land their catches in American ports, eliminating profitable markets in Nova Scotia and the French Indies. In theory, the British and French would so suffer without American trade that they would rescind their decrees and permit free trade throughout Europe once and for all. The ploy failed.[7]

The Embargo was another of the many Federal policies leading up to the War of 1812, which generated real hatred in New England for the Democrat-Republican party of Jefferson. Duxbury merchants, who were just hitting their stride on the international stage, urged that the Town voice protest to President Jefferson, which was voted during a Town Meeting in 1808. The following is taken from the letter sent to the President:

The inhabitants of the Town of Duxbury…beg leave to represent that your petitioners have hitherto depended on Commerce, Navigation and the Fisheries and the numerous arts subservient thereto for a subsistence, that the soil of this Township is sterile, and insufficient for the production of necessaries competent for the support of the people who inhabit it and that if they be much longer prohibited from following their customary avocations on the Ocean, a large proportion of them must migrate or starve.[8]

Jefferson had little sympathy for their situation. The embargo remained in effect until March 15, 1809.

The economic significance of the embargo, at least where shipbuilding in the towns of Plymouth Bay is concerned, has been exaggerated. Historian Samuel Eliot Morison observed that the embargo had a devastating economic effect on the smaller centers of shipbuilding in Massachusetts, writing:

The embargo caused greatest hardship in the smaller ports, and among small ship owners and working people dependent on shipping. Newburyport, Salem and Plymouth never recovered their former prosperity. Jefferson hastened the inevitable absorption of their commerce by Boston. Shipbuilding, with all its subsidiary industries, ceased altogether. Mechanics and master mariners had to resort to the soup kitchens…[9]

It is true that there was a significant dip in shipbuilding activities in Plymouth, Kingston, and Duxbury during the embargo. And the year 1808 must have been hard on the average fisherman or ship's carpenter. However, the embargo represented but a momentary lull for those three towns on Plymouth Bay. Indeed, shipbuilding activities immediately following the embargo reached their highest levels up to that point. All three towns showed strong activity through the 1810s, and for Duxbury and Kingston, the golden era was yet to come. The significance of the embargo to the carpenters and merchants in Plymouth County was more political than economic.

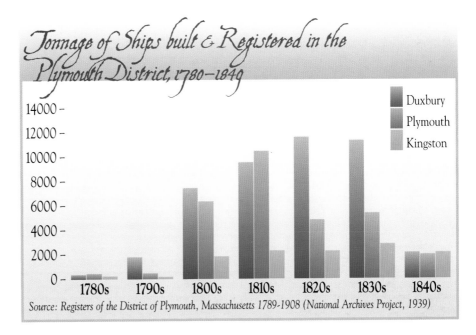

Tonnage of Ships built & Registered in the Plymouth District, 1780–1849

- Duxbury
- Plymouth
- Kingston

Source: Registers of the District of Plymouth, Massachusetts 1789-1908 (National Archives Project, 1939)

Still, determining what to do with a workforce temporarily without any work was a quandary. There was little point, during the embargo, in building vessels. The merchants in Duxbury responded by putting their carpenters to work on new houses.

And so, in 1809, the King Caesar House was completed by shipyard workers who were pleased to have jobs. King Caesar was probably just as pleased to have a fine, new mansion. Although he may well have preferred a new ship.

House and Grounds

The finished King Caesar House completed a commanding row of three Weston houses on the shore of Powder Point: the Eliphas Weston house on the east, the smaller Ezra I house in the center, and now the new house of Ezra II on the west. It bore all the elements of the popular Federal style, conveying

The Knapp family made certain Victorian alterations to King Caesar's House in the late 1880s including this unusual central staircase (near right). In the 20th century, a straight flight (far right) was installed similar to that of King Caesar's day.

Two of Frederick Knapp's daughters in early 19th-century dress in the parlor of the King Caesar House c. 1910. The girl on the right is most likely Lucia Bradford Knapp (1889-1952). The present day photo shows the c. 1820 French wallpaper still in excellent condition.

*The Knapp family dining room
in the King Caesar House,
c. 1910; and as it appears today,
representing King Caesar's era.*

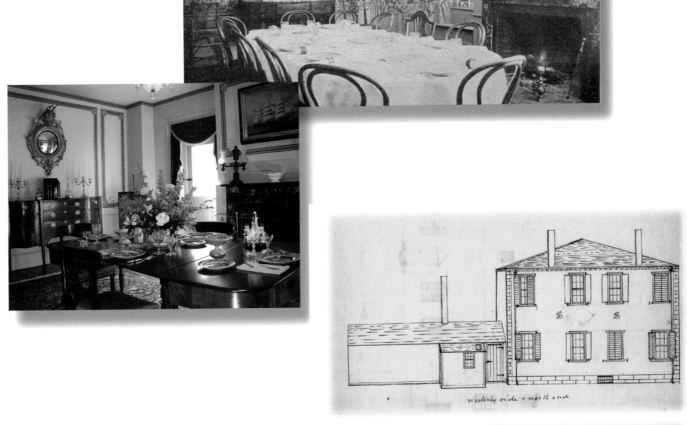

*About 1840, the King Caesar House was greatly enlarged and many of its rooms were reconfigured.
The upper sketch shows the west side of the house as constructed in 1809. The new, larger ell (lower sketch)
had more spacious workspace and quarters for household and outdoor staff, both male and female.
The woodshed and barn at left still stand. The low section of ell with only one window no longer stands, but otherwise
the house today bears virtually the same exterior appearance as in the lower sketch. Both sketches rendered c. 1840.*

The northeast chamber of the King Caesar House c. 1910 as furnished by the Knapp family. The bed and mirror pictured here are presently in the collection of the Duxbury Rural and Historical Society.

to the viewer the status and good taste of the occupants. The house was located atop a small rise and centered on the Westons' wharf, built in 1790. It was the focal point of the property, an imposing presence looming behind those at work in Westons' storehouses.

There were five buildings on the wharf at that time. After the firm closed its books, the buildings were moved off the property in the late 19th century and incorporated into other structures, some of which survive today. One was a large sail loft where sails were cut, sewn, and stored. This building was removed and attached to Dr. Reuben Peterson's barn, now a residence at 233 Powder Point Avenue. A workhouse used to grind and store salt was moved in 1866 and used as a barn next to the Captain Josephus Dawes house in the Island Creek neighborhood. This barn was eventually taken down and its timbers were used in a new house on Powder Point Avenue. Two storehouses were removed by Stephen Nye Gifford in the late 19th century and used at his cranberry bog on Temple Street. Finally, there was a counting house in which Weston and his sons must have spent much of their time while in Duxbury managing the firm's affairs.[10]

West of the house, near the formal garden, was a one-story carpenter shop. Beyond, stood the tarhouse and the massive ropewalk. Behind the house were four barns for oxen, pigs, horses, and cows as well as a chicken coop and a very large woodshed. The broad expanse of land north of the house, away from the shore and

This Spanish style steeple on the back of the King Caesar House is the center of an unusual tale. The steeple appears in the c. 1840 architectural sketches of the house. According to tradition, first documented by the Knapp family around 1930, the steeple came out of the hold of a pirate vessel that had attacked one of King Caesar's ships and been defeated. The Duxbury crew brought the steeple back to King Caesar as a trophy.

beyond the barns, was farmed in King Caesar's day to provide food for his family and workers. There were orchards, vegetable gardens, and fields of corn, beans, and potatoes. Weston also owned farms in west Duxbury and Pembroke where cattle and pigs were raised to provision his vessels.

The formal garden and house were Jerusha's domain. We can only imagine how she went about furnishing the home, as very few of the family's belongings have survived. However, good indicators of Jerusha's

A Mythical Tunnel

The most persistent myth regarding the King Caesar House is that a secret tunnel ran under the property and was used for clandestine purposes. Such tales were documented early in the 20th century in such sources as the following 1930s newspaper article:

> Dr. H.C. Bumpus has been fixing up the old Weston-Knapp mansion on King Caesar Road. He has restored the old wallpaper, which is very renowned, having been made over a hundred years ago, and is as good today as when it was put on. Amongst other things he has run across is a cellar situated in one of the old sheds back of the main house. This cellar is quite sizeable and its walls are of stone and very thick. Above this cellar, which was about eight or ten feet deep, was a ring bolt evidently employed for lowering things into it. Here undoubtedly, was the secret cellar where goods from the Far East were placed secretly to avoid duties.
>
> The Weston ships were anchored in the Cow Yard and the story goes that at night these goods were rowed up the bay and placed into this secret cellar, thus avoiding the duties. It has also been claimed that this story is untrue, and this was an ice house, but why, if this is so, should there not have been some drain whereby the ice water could have been carried away which was not the case...There is also a tale that this cellar was connected with the water by a tunnel. This is manifestly untrue because no tunnel could have been built which would not have been filled with water at the higher tides. The shed has been torn down, the whole cellar filled in, and over the place where the smuggled goods were concealed, motor cars now travel.[11]

The King Caesar House c. 1937. Once again falling into disrepair after the deaths of Frederick and Fanny Knapp in 1932 and 1934, the house was bought in 1937 by Dr. Hermon Carey Bumpus (1863-1943), former Director of the American Museum of Natural History in New York. Bumpus acquired several historic houses throughout New England for the purpose of refurbishing them. The Bumpus family owned the property until 1945.

Photograph courtesy of the Library of Congress Historic American Buildings Survey.

Cars still travel over the mysterious cellar along what is now the driveway behind the house. The cellar, dating to about 1840 when the house was enlarged, is labeled on plans drafted in that year as an ice cellar. It probably never contained anything more interesting than that. There is no evidence to suggest that Weston was ever involved in smuggling and he was not interested in the Far East trade.

Frederick B. Knapp, who purchased the house from the Weston family and converted the estate into a successful boys' preparatory school, used to allow his students to dig for the mythical tunnel from time to time. No doubt, after getting a few feet down, the students figured out that the joke was on them.

expensive tastes are the surviving wallpapers in the house, which date from the early 19th century. In the west parlor is a scenic treatment called "Le Parc Francaise" by Jaquemart and Bernard, produced about 1820. The paper in the sitting room, called "Les Incas," was inspired by the 1777 novel of the same name written by Jean Francois Marmontel. It was first produced by Leroy and Dufour in 1818. Both papers are in remarkable condition.

In 1840, the house underwent a considerable transformation. The dining room was enlarged and an ornate marble fireplace was installed. A wing housing a new kitchen and a dairy room was constructed off the west side. The short kitchen ell off the rear, originally one story, was greatly enlarged with new quarters for male and female servants, a carriage house, washrooms, and water closets. Carpenters reconfigured the central staircase and the bedchambers upstairs. The renovation took place at the peak of King Caesar's prosperity, at the same time as the construction of his largest ships. At age 67 Weston apparently desired that his house mirror the successes of his firm.

Powder Point School for Boys

Students and faculty of the Powder Point School for Boys c. 1905. Frederick B. Knapp is in the back row, fourth from the left.

On September 1, 1886, Frederick and Fanny Knapp, "left Cambridge about 9 in morning having done some last college work…drove Taffy (their horse) to Duxbury and spent the night at Aunt Hatty Bradford's. The men," Knapp wrote in his journal, "are already at work repairing our house at Powder Point." [12]

Having made up their minds to establish a preparatory school for boys, the Knapps had bought, just days earlier, the old King Caesar estate, now rather run down. Given the attractive location of the property and the many outbuildings ideal for conversion to classrooms and gymnasiums, it was the perfect site. Coincidentally, Frederick Knapp was related to Jerusha Bradford Weston (his great-grandaunt), a fact that probably contributed to his fondness for the property.

King Caesar's son, Alden B. Weston, was the last of the Westons to live in the house. Alden had married late in life, but his wife died before him and he lived alone in the King Caesar House for 11 years. The money earned during the Weston firm's heyday largely gone, Alden had difficulty maintaining the estate. After his death in 1880, the house passed to his nephews and nieces, the children of his older brother Gershom.

These grandchildren of King Caesar, with two exceptions, all lived outside of Duxbury and had little interest in moving into the estate. The two granddaughters who lived in Duxbury were both unmarried and could not take on such a responsibility.

And then there was the issue of the title. It was rumored that Alden had bequeathed the house to the First Parish Church, although a copy of the will was never found. This was enough to deter many from getting involved in the property. So the house sat, largely unoccupied, from 1880 until 1886.

Powder Point Hall, above, the main dormitory of the preparatory school, was constructed in 1893, burned in 1913 and was replaced by a new dormitory shown below. The structure stood on the site of the house of Eliphas Weston, Ezra II's grandfather. In 1931 the building was purchased by the National Sailors Home. It was torn down in 1975.

The questionable title did not faze the provider of Knapp's insurance, however, and that was sufficient in Knapp's view to go ahead with the purchase.[13]

Knapp set about making improvements to the house and grounds. He had a setback on the night of December 30, four months after moving in, when he was awakened by pounding on his door. The Ezra Weston I house, known as "the Cottage," was ablaze. Neighbors quickly assembled to help fight the conflagration. The wind was out of the northeast and leaping flames began to lick at the King Caesar House. Fearing that both houses might be lost, Knapp worked fiercely, seriously endangering himself in the fight. The Cottage was lost. Fortunately no one was in it at the time. The King Caesar house was saved with only minor damage. This traumatic event later motivated Knapp to become chief of Duxbury's Volunteer Fire Department and advocate for the purchase of fire fighting equipment.

The most notable Victorian alteration the Knapps made to the King Caesar House was this verandah. The windmill stood behind the house.

A new, larger cottage that was built on roughly the same site still stands today. It served numerous purposes, primarily as a residence for faculty. The kitchen ell of the old Ezra I house, which was spared by the fire, was converted into a chemistry laboratory. Knapp had playing fields laid out where King Caesar's cornfields had been. A huge dormitory was constructed on the east side of the estate where the Eliphas Weston house once stood. With a capacity of 75 students and 9 faculty by the 1910s, the school was a great success.

Knapp's diaries tell of many happy days in the King Caesar House: Thanksgiving dinners after which each of his four children were given turns on the scale to see how much they'd eaten, Christmas mornings with scavenger hunts for oranges and treats, and jovial birthday parties. He served as headmaster of the school for 23 years until the death of his 19-year old son, Eric, of a "brain fever," probably resulting from either encephalitis or meningitis. Knapp was so affected by his son's death that he resigned, but he continued to live on in the headmaster's house with his family. He died in 1932, a beloved figure in the community.

Fanny Hall Knapp (1854-1934) in the sitting room of the King Caesar House c. 1890. Frederick Knapp's wife played an active role in the selection of a campus for their planned preparatory school. After Knapp retired, she was involved in their extensive pursuit of real estate interests in Duxbury. During the Knapp's time, the French wallpaper for which this room is known was moved upstairs. The paper was moved back in 1965.

CHAPTER FIVE

A Reformation

There would be changes following the death of Ezra Weston I.

Ezra Weston II set high goals for the firm and pursued them vigorously. The most significant change was the immediate acquisition of larger vessels. In part, this was a sign of the times. According to historian Samuel Eliot Morison, there was "a superstition prevalent until about 1830 that a vessel over 500 tons was unsafe and would break in a heavy sea." Relieved of this superstition, Massachusetts shipbuilders in the 1830s began turning out very large cargo vessels.[1]

Exhibiting a passion for conducting business on the largest possible scale, King Caesar joined this trend with gusto, eventually commissioning New England's largest merchant ship (prior to 1841) and amassing one of its largest fleets. This trend, and others beginning almost immediately after Ezra I's death, heralded a new era for the firm.

Merchant of Boston

In the 1820s, Weston began to shift his commercial operations to Boston. As previously noted, even in the earliest days, the Westons depended on resources in Boston that were not available closer to home. Their larger vessels had always used that port as their base, as Duxbury and Plymouth lacked harbors of sufficient depth and markets to support the scope of their trade. While Weston's shipyard, ropewalk, and mill in Duxbury continued to support his fleet, his counting house in Boston increasingly became the center of his affairs.

In 1818, the Westons established a counting house on Boston's Long Wharf. They occupied several different offices on the wharf until finally settling in number 29 in 1828, where they remained for the next seven years. The Weston counting rooms were on the second floor above Kent & Bates, a business owned in part by William V. Kent of Duxbury whom King Caesar sometimes employed as an overseas business agent.[2]

Alden B. Weston, the middle son and head of clerical affairs, managed the Weston office full time. Alden took up residence in Boston nearly year-round beginning in 1827 at age 22. For five years he lived on Brattle Street, in the core of Boston's commercial district, just up the hill from Faneuil Hall. Later he moved to a boarding house on fashionable Pearl Street. For decades Alden spent most of his time in Boston. Although residing in Duxbury part-time, he did not fully settle back into his father's home on Powder Point until after the firm closed its books in 1857.

Boston's Long Wharf c. 1855. The counting rooms of the firm of E. Weston & Son (later E. Weston) were located here from 1818 until 1835.

Photograph courtesy of the Bostonian Society.

King Caesar seems to have divided his time more evenly between Duxbury and Boston. By 1828 he had established an address in a boarding house at 3 Bath Street, now the site of Post Office Square, just up the street from Alden's Pearl Street residence. Ezra II's address is later given as within the Franklin Hotel (a rendering of which survives), a boarding house on Merchant's Row near Faneuil Hall. This was his residence while in Boston from 1828 to 1835.[3]

The notebook King Caesar kept in the 1830s indicates frequent trips back and forth to Boston, a sort of precursor to the contemporary suburban commute. Weston's packet schooners often sailed back and forth to the city. Unlike his father who used these packets to catch a ride from time to time, the

Ezra Weston II kept a room in this boarding house on Merchant's Row just north of Faneuil Hall from 1828 to 1835.

In the background of this Boston waterfront view is Commercial Wharf c. 1873. Completed in 1835, this imposing wharf housed the Weston firm's counting rooms at numbers 37 and 38 from 1835 to 1857.

Photograph courtesy of the Massachusetts Historical Society.

A present day view of the wharf is shown at far right.

younger King Caesar evidently preferred travel overland. He kept horses at a "halfway house" in Hanover along the Bay Road. Leaving Duxbury in the middle of the night, Weston would drive his chaise to Hanover along the Bay Road (roughly the same course traversed by today's Route 53) to change horses before dawn. He was probably in the habit of driving at a good clip given the necessity for this stopover. From there he proceeded on to Hingham where he took advantage of the new steamboats plying Boston harbor. One such steamboat was the *General Lincoln*, named after Hingham's Revolutionary War hero, Benjamin Lincoln, which departed Hingham at 6:30 a.m. and arrived at Liverpool Wharf in Boston at 9 a.m. The fare was 37½ cents. In all, the "commute" probably took more than five hours. According to family tradition, Weston often made this trip simply to conduct a single day's business, repeating the same arduous process at the end of the day. It is no wonder that his son Alden preferred his Boston residence.[4]

Weston became involved in several Boston banks and businesses, owning shares in Long Wharf and the Commercial Bank on State Street among others. Beginning in 1825 he was a Director of the Merchants Insurance Company, later known as

Brattle Street, Boston, c. 1850. Alden B. Weston, manager of the Weston counting rooms in Boston, lived here from 1827 to 1831. The street is now the site of Boston's City Hall Plaza.

Photograph courtesy of the Bostonian Society.

the United States Insurance Company. He was appointed Secretary in 1828.[5]

In 1835, with the firm reaching its heyday, Weston became one of the first merchants to occupy offices on Boston's new Commercial Wharf. This huge granite building with its commodious counting rooms was a great symbol of Boston's commercial success. It became home to some of the city's most distinguished merchant houses. As Boston historian William S. Rossiter observed, "Commercial [Wharf] was the first of the New North End structures, and far exceeded anything of the kind in Boston for its imposing massiveness…It was a high toned wharf in those days, and if a fishing smack or a lobster boat stuck its nose into the dock, it would have been fired out instanter."[6]

The firm occupied numbers 37 and 38 Commercial Wharf for 22 years until it ceased operation. Wharf hands here tied up Duxbury's finest vessels, Weston's growing fleet.

The Builders

Examining the full spectrum of vessel acquisition throughout the history of the Weston firm demonstrates just how dramatically Ezra Weston II launched into the construction of a large fleet after his father's death. The years 1823 and 1824 show a curious pause in the firm's shipbuilding, the only lull since the War of 1812. Given the difficulties Weston had in settling his father's estate, this hiatus must have been necessary in order to straighten out the firm's affairs

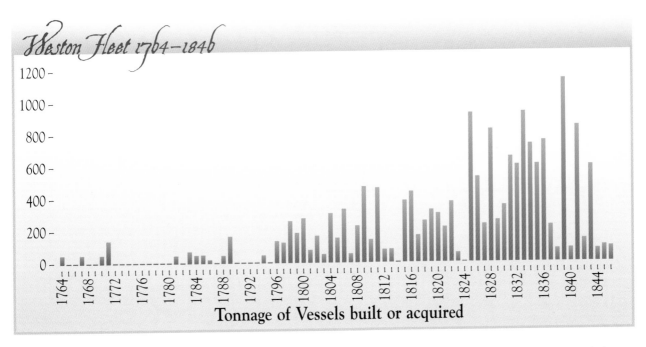

Weston Fleet 1764–1846

1200 –
1000 –
800 –
600 –
400 –
200 –
0 –

1764 1768 1772 1776 1780 1784 1788 1792 1796 1800 1804 1808 1812 1816 1820 1824 1828 1832 1836 1840 1844

Tonnage of Vessels built or acquired

and to set new priorities. That accomplished, Weston immediately proceeded to commission new vessels far larger than those acquired by his father. This burst of activity continued throughout the 1830s, facilitated by the eventual construction of a new shipyard owned by Weston on the Bluefish River.

Determined to acquire a bigger and better fleet, Weston first had to find the right men to build it. For reasons unknown, he left behind the master builder that his father had employed. Up until this point, many of the Westons' vessels had been

*Launched in Duxbury in 1822, the 162-ton **Herald** was the last vessel built for the Westons by master carpenter Benjamin Prior. She was employed primarily in trade to Smyrna and Trieste. She is shown here entering the port of Trieste under Captain Martin Waterman. After 12 years of Weston ownership, she was sold on October 21, 1834 in Boston to Robert Brookhouse of Salem.*

constructed in a shipyard at Harden Hill Bay in South Duxbury. It was known as the "Navy Yard" because of it tremendous size. The yard was owned by shipwright Benjamin Prior. According to tradition, Prior built much of the Weston fleet here in the 1810s but his name is only listed with one on the Plymouth ship registers—the brig *Herald* launched in 1822. It was the last vessel Prior constructed for the Weston firm. Either unable or unwilling to build the sort of vessels the new King Caesar desired, Prior was no longer involved in Weston activities after Ezra I's death. Ezra II purchased the yard from Prior in 1822. He had, however, no master carpenter to superintend the yard.

Seeking a new builder, King Caesar made a choice in 1825 that was atypical of the firm's history and demonstrated his apparent desire to try new avenues in pursuit of new goals. The North River formed the boundary between Scituate (part of which is now Norwell) and Marshfield and was the site of numerous active shipyards. Some of them had been in existence for more than a century, producing vessels that were mainly sold to owners in Boston. The Westons had looked in this direction before, in 1820, when they commissioned the brig *Margaret* from Scituate shipbuilders Seth and Samuel Foster.

Ezra Weston II evidently liked the quality of the vessel. He commissioned the Fosters to build three more in 1825 and 1826 while he searched for a new builder in Duxbury. With so many shipyards in Duxbury by this time, it was unusual for Weston to seek out North River builders. Given their reputation, though, it is

*The **Lagoda** is the only vessel owned by Ezra Weston II known to have been photographed. She is shown here at Merrill's Wharf in New Bedford, c. 1870, during her whaling days. The New Bedford Whaling Museum today features an enormous half-scale model of the **Lagoda** in its Jonathan Bourne room.*
The boy right of center provides a good sense of scale.

Photograph courtesy of the
New Bedford Whaling Museum..

The **Lagoda** sketched by marine artist George C. Wales. Built in 1826 by Seth and Samuel Foster in what is now Norwell, the 340-ton **Lagoda** was owned by King Caesar until 1832. She was later a part of New Bedford's whaling fleet and is here depicted as a whaler.

Photograph courtesy of the Peabody Essex Museum.

not surprising that the Fosters attracted Weston's attention. At the time, the Foster yard, known as the Wanton Shipyard in what is now Norwell (then known as South Scituate), was one of the most successful on the North River. In 1817 the Fosters turned out an amazing six vessels, a record for yards in that region.[7]

The North River vessels were exceedingly durable. L. Vernon Briggs, who wrote the *History of Shipbuilding on the North River*, was able to track down the whereabouts of several North River vessels still afloat at the time of his writing in 1889. The *Pioneer*, which Weston commissioned in 1825 and owned until about 1830, was still in operation more than 50 years later.

Even more remarkable was the *Lagoda*, built in the Foster yard in 1826. She was named for the Russian Lake Ladoga but the letters were inadvertently switched by the men who painted her transom. Weston owned her for nearly seven years, employing her in trade with European ports including Antwerp and Havre until February 25, 1833 when he sold her to Boston merchant William Oliver. She was later purchased by Jonathan Bourne of New Bedford and converted to a whaling ship. Bourne owned her for 45 years. The *Lagoda* had a narrow scrape in 1871 when an early cold snap and shifting winds caught a large number of American whaling ships by surprise in the Bering Straights. As ice began to pack in around the vessels, dozens had to be abandoned. The *Lagoda*, beating a southerly course, barely made it out of the Straights in time. She then assisted in gathering up the crews of the abandoned ships.

After New Bedford merchant William Lewis bought her, the *Lagoda* continued to sail the Pacific as a whaler. Finally, she was sold to Japanese owners who employed her as a coal supply hulk for the Japanese whaling fleets in the 1890s. Sometime after 1899 she burned and broke apart in Kanagawa, Japan. Such was the amazing lifespan of more than 75 years for a ship built on a small river in Norwell, Massachusetts.[8]

Weston's transactions with the Fosters were short-lived. The South Scituate builders supplied fine new vessels in a period during which Weston's shipbuilding activities were in transition. But by 1826, King Caesar had found his builder. When Samuel Hall and Ezra Weston II met, it was a providential occurrence with

The first vessel built for Weston by 26-year-old master carpenter Samuel Hall, the 174-ton brig **Ganges** is here shown in 1826 entering the port of Smyrna.

significant ramifications for both men. Hall, then 26, was a young man who showed astounding talent as a shipwright. Weston, 53, was just the sort of established mentor Hall needed.

Samuel Hall was born in Marshfield in 1800 and served an apprenticeship in the yard of Deacon Elijah Barstow in Hanover. After completing his training, Hall went to Medford and then to Camden, Maine in search of work. Things were evidently not to his liking there, for he returned to Marshfield in 1825 and began building small vessels with his brothers Luke and William.[9]

Weston took Hall on as master carpenter of his shipyard in 1826. By placing such a young man in the key position of overseeing the design and construction of his vessels, Weston took a risk. The old salts working in the Navy Yard must have bristled at the notion of taking orders from a fresh fish. But Weston recognized something promising about Hall.

King Caesar's gamble paid off. Hall constructed some of the most superior vessels owned by the Weston firm, creating the new fleet King Caesar envisioned. Hall built 14 ships for Weston between 1826 and 1836, beginning with the brig *Ganges*. When the *Mattakeesett* (481 tons) was launched in 1833, it was one of the largest vessels in New England, the second largest built in the customs district of Plymouth up to that time. Nearly every one of the Hall vessels was a gem of the Weston fleet, each used by the firm for an average of 9 years and some as long as 20 years. Thanks to Hall, Weston's fleet, already possessing a fine reputation, became a widely known paragon. Boston newspapers noted in salutary terms the efforts of the magnate of the South Shore. The following article from the *Boston Gazette* was so enthusiastic in its praise that it attracted attention in Baltimore and was re-printed there:

> **Ship Building at Duxbury.** – *The art of ship building has been brought to great perfection by our enterprising neighbors of Duxbury. A few days since was launched from the yard of Mr. Ezra Weston of the town, of which Mr. Samuel Hall is master carpenter, the fine ship* **Undine**. *This ship is of the tea-kettle model, and in every respect is said to be a first rate vessel—she will be commanded by Capt. Nathaniel Weston, Jr. The* **Undine** *is the sixth square-rigged vessel that has been built by Mr. E. Weston since 1829—all of which are of the first class. Amongst*

*these, are the well-known ships **Julian, Renown**, and **Joshua Bates**. The latter is now on her passage from London to Boston, and we hear is intended as a regular packet between the two places. There are now on the stocks in Duxbury two ships and a brig, and others are to be raised this fall… The Duxbury built vessels are inferior to none, either in respect to beauty or goodness, they always command the first freights, and if exposed for sale, the first prices.*[10]

At times, Weston found himself surprised at the speed with which Hall turned out vessels and a bit taken aback by the growth of his own fleet. In 1833, he received a letter from one of his captains requesting instructions—freights in his current port were extremely dull, he complained. As noted above, Weston vessels were typically offered the highest freights, and King Caesar rarely settled for anything else. If rates in a particular port were low, a Weston captain found himself in a difficult bind of waiting in port for freights to improve, at considerable expense, or, less desirable, leaving the port in ballast, which would mean a deficit on the voyage. Weston, who usually had quite specific instructions to his captains as to type of cargo, consignee, and rate, was uncharacteristically at a loss in this case. He replied to the captain,

> *I hope you will be able to find some employment for the **Minerva** in preference to hauling her up. If a freight to New Orleans in the amount of $2,000, would it not be well to accept it? We missed it very much not accepting the offer we had in Boston last spring…. I do not know what is to be done with the ship. And to add to my troubles, on the 14th Mr. Hall intends launching another ship—350 tons—called the **St. Lawrence**. A very superior ship you may depend.*[11]

Levi Sampson (1783-1867) was one of Duxbury's successful shipbuilders. His yard was adjacent to Weston's Ten Acre Yard, just east of the Bluefish River Bridge. He built primarily for Thomas Lamb of Boston, but he also built two vessels for Ezra Weston II in 1822 and 1825 while Weston re-structured the management of his own shipyard.

The largest, and last, ship Hall built for Weston was the *Eliza Warwick* (530 tons) in 1836. This was an unusual cooperative venture for Weston, partly financed and owned by merchant Abraham Warwick of Richmond, Virginia. Weston, conducting frequent business in Richmond loading freights of tobacco, struck up a friendship with the Warwick family of that city. Accustomed to sole ownership, King Caesar had to remind himself repeatedly in his notebook to list Warwick as co-owner in various papers.

In 1834, Weston took a bold step. For decades the firm's vessels had been built in the Navy Yard at Harden Hill. It was far from Weston's headquarters on Powder Point and, more importantly, from his wharf where vessels had to be hauled for outfitting. Seeing an opportunity, Weston purchased land on the south bank of

During the 1810s, much of the Weston fleet was built in a shipyard owned by Benjamin Prior at Harden Hill Bay. The south side of the bay is here shown after the shipbuilding days, c. 1890.

the Bluefish River near the Harmony Bridge constructed through his father's efforts 31 years before. Here Weston created the Ten Acre Yard. Significantly larger than the yard at Harden Hill, the Ten Acre Yard had the capacity for the simultaneous construction of two vessels. Samuel Hall built four vessels here from 1834-36. Later, the largest ships of Weston's fleet would be built here.

At the time, there were six shipyards packed in around the mouth of the Bluefish River. Close by Ezra Weston's new yard were those of Levi Sampson on the west (who Weston commissioned to build two ships) and Luther Turner on the east. The yards were so close that when a fire broke out in Levi Sampson's yard in 1834, it threatened the *Admittance* then on the stocks in Weston's yard.[12]

*The ship **Julian**, launched in Duxbury in 1828. At an ambitious 356 tons, she was the second vessel constructed for Weston by Samuel Hall. At the time, she was the largest in the Weston fleet. She was commanded by Captains Benjamin Smith and Martin Waterman until sold in 1834 to Thomas Biddle of New Bedford for a whaler, a common outcome for Weston vessels. She is shown here as a whaler.*

Image courtesy of the
New Bedford Whaling Museum.

After a successful ten-year association with Weston, Hall decided in 1837 to strike out on his own, opening a shipyard just north of the old Weston Navy Yard. He built there for two years. Then, tiring of the limitations of the shallow bay, Hall moved to East Boston in 1839, building one of the first shipyards in what would become a center of shipbuilding known throughout the world. Between 1839 and 1860 Samuel Hall's East Boston yard turned out 110 vessels, including the 1,261-ton *Surprise*, in 1850 the first clipper ship built in Boston. Clipper ships were already in high demand in New York, and with their sharp lines, sleek hulls, and massive expanses of canvas, they soon became the most desirable form of merchant vessel, especially for sending a cargo quickly around the Horn to San Francisco.

In an ironic twist, Hall, aged 50 and an experienced master builder, had to tolerate the brilliant young designer of the *Surprise* engaged by its future owners. Samuel Harte Pook, who at 23 had led an accelerated career as a naval architect, found it difficult to work with the older shipbuilder. Perhaps forgetting the chance that had been given him by Ezra Weston, Hall was irritated by Pook's modern and thoroughly ingenious ideas on ship design. They eventually managed to get along, however, and their collaboration was a tremendous success. The *Surprise*, impressively launched fully rigged, broke the record by which clippers were measured completing the run to San Francisco in 96 days and 15 hours. She was the first of many famous clippers Samuel Hall built.[13]

Hall's departure in 1836 left Weston without a builder until Samuel Cushing took over in 1837. Cushing, about whom little information survives, certainly possessed considerable vision and ability. He built the great giants of the Weston fleet: the *Oneco*, the *Manteo*, and the *Hope*.

Vessels built 1825–1849 and registered in the District of Plymouth, Top Owners

Name	Residence of Owners	Number of Vessels Registered	Tonnage of Vessels Registered	Percentage of Total Registered
Ezra Weston and Sons	Duxbury	27	8,494	20%
Charles and Reuben Drew	Duxbury	18	5,212	12%
Joseph Holmes and Sons	Kingston	10	2,782	6%
John Sever	Kingston	9	2,600	6%
Levi Sampson & Thomas Lamb	Duxbury & Boston	7	2,356	5%
Ezra & Ephraim Finney, Benjamin Barnes	Plymouth	7	1,977	5%
Thomas, Abraham & Daniel Jackson	Plymouth	6	1,781	4%
Isaac & Thomas Hedge, Jacob Covington	Plymouth	5	1,451	3%
Seth Sprague	Duxbury	5	1,108	3%
Henry B. & William Sampson, et. al.	Duxbury	4	837	2%
Total		**104**	**29,421**	**68%**

Source: Ship Registers of the District of Plymouth, Massachusetts 1789-1908 (National Archives Project, 1939)

With this sharp increase in his shipbuilding activity, King Caesar dramatically widened the gap between himself and other fleet owners in Plymouth County during the second quarter of the 19th century. Whereas in the first quarter of the century, 7% of the vessels registered in the Plymouth Customs district belonged to Weston, by the 1840s he owned 20% of the region's tonnage. In 1825, Weston was the leader, but only by a 2% margin . Now he had far exceeded his competitors, as most Plymouth district merchant houses of the 1830s and 1840s showed little or no growth in terms of percentage of tonnage owned. The second quarter of the 19th century also saw a consolidation of ownership under the top merchant houses. Whereas the top ten houses owned 37% of tonnage in the first quarter of the century, they owned 68% in the second quarter.

Of course, to take charge of this fine, new fleet, King Caesar needed master mariners of the first rate. In the late 1820s, with many of the sea captains of his own generation retiring, Weston faced a challenge in attracting new masters for his vessels.

Captains

For Captain Ichabod Simmons, 1832 was a tough year.

On February 3 he left Hampton Roads, master of King Caesar's brig *Levant*, one of the North River vessels commissioned by Weston in 1825. Taking his departure from the lighthouse on Cape Henry, Simmons made a course for Antwerp. Five days out, he discovered that the brig was leaking. This was not uncommon in older vessels, and to some extent it was to be expected, especially if caught in a heavy sea. Devoting manpower to the pumps would usually contain the problem until a port was reached.

The *Levant*, however, was not in a heavy sea. And the leak was getting worse. "Brig leaking bad," Simmons noted in his log five days later. Still, as long as they were spared rough weather, there was no reason to expect that they could not reach Antwerp.

On Sunday morning, February 19, the *Levant* hit rough weather. That evening, Simmons noted in his log, "at 11 am, shipped a sea [the brig went under a wave], parted the boat grips, sent her down to leeward and carried away the larboard bulwarks and washed overboard a top mast studensail. [The wave] knocked in the galley and did other damage. Ship very leaky."

The storm continued for two days. The following night, Simmons wrote, "At midnight, the wind started to the north and freshened. At 2 am, shipped a heavy

Sketched in 1832 in the logbook of Captain Ichabod Simmons, the brig **Levant** *was launched about 1825.*

sea over our starboard quarter. Broke the davys [davits, or arms used to hold anchors and boats in place], carried off the small boat and did other damage. [The gale] blowed the jib loose and tore it all to pieces and carried away the man ropes from the bowsprit and staysail netting. Larboard bulwarks and ports chiefly gone. Leaking bad. One pump going all of the time."

On the next day, there was no relief. "Continues to blow hard and a very bad sea. Brig labours hard and ships a great deal of water. Leaking bad."

On Wednesday the storm finally let up and Simmons set all hands to work repairing the extensive damage. Then, he estimated their position in the Atlantic and set a course for the closest land, the Isle of Wight in the English Channel, abandoning their plans to go to Antwerp. For a week the *Levant* labored along, each day's log entry concluding with, "brig leaking…"

Finally, on Thursday, March 1, the brig made land at the Isle of Wight. But there was no pilot to meet them off the island, as there normally should have been, to guide them into the harbor of Cowes. Standing in toward the harbor, trying to attract attention, the *Levant* hove to and stood off again, repeating the attempt three times. After a day of this, a pilot finally arrived and guided them into the port and they came to anchor.

Captain Simmons immediately brought on board a surveyor to assess the severity of the damage and determine whether they could proceed to Antwerp. The surveyor determined that the brig was taking on five inches of water per hour in

calm water. The *Levant* spent about a month in Cowes as repairs were made. May found captain and his crew finally at their destination of Antwerp. However, it was not the end of the *Levant's* troubles.

After a brief stop in St. Ubes in Portugal, the *Levant* set sail homeward for Duxbury, departing on May 23. By June 1 they had reached the Azores and had a pleasant stopover of five days, proceeding homeward again on June 6. Four days later, the wind shifted, a heavy gale blew in, and the sea began breaking over the brig repeatedly. On June 14, tragedy struck.

"Stiff breezes from SWS. Heavy squalls at midnight. Double reefed the topsails. At 2 am, the wind shifted to the north. Wore ship and lost Edmond Crosley off the main yard. Blowing so heavy and a heavy sea that we could not get the boat out. Hove aback and sent overboard plank. Wore ship several times, but could not find him. Split the jib and foresail. Took them in."

The brig suffered further damage over the next two days.

"At 2 am, shipped a sea over our larboard beam. Carried away the bulwark and stove the caboose house and sent the caboose down to leeward.... The sea continually breaking over us did considerable damage to hull and rigging. At midnight, the wind moderated. Got the foresail and close reeft fore topsail on her. All hands employed in mending the cook's galley and other damages."

Captain Simeon Soule (1790-1843) was one of Weston's most dependable master mariners. He spent a total of 10 years at sea on Weston vessels, most notably the brig Neptune from 1829-1834. Portrait c. 1830.

Having survived the storm, the *Levant* crawled toward the Grand Banks. The crew sighted Cape Ann in the afternoon of July 9. By 7 the next morning they passed the Gurnet at Plymouth Bay, coming to anchor off Clark's Island at 9 o'clock. Captain Simmons, no doubt dreading the tasks ahead, disembarked to explain to King Caesar that his brig was badly in need of repair and to convey the sad news to Crosley's family.[14]

Captain Benjamin Smith (1784-1848) was master of Weston's brig Pioneer and the ship Julian, the flagship of the fleet at the time.

The voyage is a good illustration of the conditions under which a master mariner was expected to do

business. A capable master had to be able to face such harrowing experiences with confidence and good judgment. Once in port, no matter how difficult the voyage, he had to conduct transactions shrewdly, overcoming challenges of language, customs, and law.

Like all fleet owners, Ezra Weston depended on resourceful men to take charge of his vessels. Concurrent with the resumption of shipbuilding activities in 1825, Weston brought on a handful of new master mariners who would be key players in his business activities. This was followed by the engagement of a larger group in the years between 1831 and 1834, a core of talented, capable, loyal ship captains who would continue to work for the Weston firm for the next 14 to 16 years.

As he did with young shipbuilder Samuel Hall, Ezra II was willing to follow his instincts and to take risks in bringing in new talent where his captains were concerned. To his credit, Weston seemed to have a knack for gathering about him excellent men whom he could trust to do well for his fleet. In so doing, he sometimes ignored long-standing maritime traditions. As Laurence Bradford, naval engineer and Duxbury historian, learned from a first-hand source,

> *It so chanced that Mr. Weston employed a certain captain who the seafaring community thought had not passed through the required lines of preparation and sent a protest to Mr. Weston, who replied that it made no difference to him where his captains came from or what their training had been, or whether they had been to sea at all. If they could sail his ships to a profit, then he wanted them, otherwise he didn't.*[15]

In the late 1820s, with the construction of a new fleet of larger vessels underway, Weston encouraged the continuing involvement of two young men who had first worked for the firm toward the end of Ezra I's life: Simeon Soule and Martin Waterman. In 1825 he added Benjamin Smith and Seth F. Sprague (a distant cousin of the older shipbuilder Seth Sprague). On this group Weston relied during the 1820s as his premier master mariners.

Joining the Weston firm in the early 1830s was a roster of eight new master mariners who were among the most dependable in the company. After operating some of Weston's smaller vessels, these men went on to serve as masters of the giants of the fleet in the later 1830s and early 1840s. Foremost among them was Joseph Cummings, serving 14 years aboard ship, who first distinguished himself as master of the *Ceres*. Later, he was appointed to the new brig *Smyrna* and then the *Mattakeesett* toward the end of that venerable ship's career. Lewis Peterson served as master of seven vessels for the firm. Zara Higgins and Freeman Soule also belonged to this group. After skillfully commanding the *Undine* and the large ship *Admittance*, Soule was granted the ultimate honor Weston could bestow. In 1841 Soule took charge of the new ship *Hope*, Weston's largest vessel.

There were new masters in the twilight years of the firm from 1843 to 1857 when King Caesar's sons managed the fleet's affairs. Notable among these were Joshua Drew, who for fully 13 years would be linked with the *Oneco*, the second largest ship in the fleet, and Gershom B. Weston II, King Caesar's oldest grandson (the only grandchild to play a role in the firm) who was master of the *Hope* and the *Oneco* after King Caesar's death. For the most part, the later masters had brief terms of service.

At least 80 men were placed in charge of Weston vessels from 1830 to 1856. The following chart lists some of the more significant, the longevity of their involvement (more than five years aboard the firm's vessels) indicating that they were highly regarded.

*Captain Gershom Bradford Weston II (1821-1887), shown c. 1860, was Ezra Weston II's first grandchild. After King Caesar's death, he was master of some of the fleet's largest vessels, including the **Hope** and the **Oneco**. Weston later became a wharfinger, residing during the 1880s in South Boston.*

Photograph courtesy of William Bradford Drury.

Sailing as a master mariner for King Caesar was a challenging experience. Weston did not take a laissez-faire attitude where his fleet was concerned. His orders to his master mariners were highly detailed and specific, indicating a sharp knowledge of market conditions in various ports. This was especially true in his later years by which time he had built up a large cadre of business contacts and agents in various ports, particularly in the United States and England. Weston depended on these contacts to convey his

Important Weston Master Mariners, 1820–1856 [16]

Captain	Years Aboard Weston Vessel as Master	Beginning	Ending	Vessels
Simeon Soule	10	1818	1834	Collector, 1818- Dray, 1825-1826 Ganges, 1826-1828 Ceres, 1828-1829 Neptune, 1829-1834
Martin Waterman	7	1820	1833	Margaret, 1820-1822 Herald, 1823-1825 Julian, c. 1830-1832 Renown, 1830
Seth F. Sprague	11	1825	1839	Smyrna,1st 1825-1829 Renown, 1830-1832 Minerva, 1832-1835 Vandalia, 1835-1838 Mattakeesett, 1838-1839
Benjamin Smith	5	1825	c. 1830	Pioneer, 1825-1828 Julian, 1828-c.1830
Zara Higgins	9	c. 1831	1841	Malaga, c.1831-1832 Herald, 1832 Messenger, 1834-1836 Mattakeesett, 1836-1841 Ceres, 1832-1833
Joseph Cummings	14	1832	1848	Herald, 1832-1834 Ceres, 1834-1836 Neptune, 1836-1839 Smyrna, 2nd, 1839-1843 Minerva, 1844 Mattakeesett, 1846-1848
Lewis Peterson	7	1833	1849	Levant, 1833-1834 Trenton, 1836-1837 Oriole, 1838 Lion, 1842-1843 Smyrna, 2nd, 1844-1845 Lion, 1845-1846 Mattakeesett, 1849
Freeman Soule	10	1834	1848	Undine, 1834-1836 Admittance, 1837 Hope, 1841-1848
Joshua Drew	13	1839	1852	Oneco, 1839-1843 Manteo, 1843-1844 Oneco, 1844-1852
Gershom B. Weston II	5	1843	1855	Mattakeesett, 1843-1844 Hope, 1848-1850 Oneco, 1854-1855

correspondence to his ship captains and supply them with advice and brokerage services. Such tight management was an important characteristic of Weston's business approach.

Correspondence sent to Captain David Cushman in the early months of 1842 demonstrates this. As master of the *Undine*, seeking a cargo in Charleston, Cushman received weekly letters from Weston dictating specific rates at which to trade and urging expediency. Referring often to "our" advice, the letters are not in King Caesar's hand, indicating that there is another individual involved in direction at this stage, possibly Alden B. Weston or another key clerk.

On April 29, King Caesar instructed, "Sir, we have letters from Charleston today saying that freight has declined and extremely dull. Therefore think you had better accept [a cargo] at Richmond…But if you cannot obtain a freight at Richmond at my limits, you will proceed direct to New Orleans, for it's of no use to stop at Charleston. Our friend at New Orleans is Louis H. Gale, Esq."

*Captain David Cushman (1807-1878) spent most of his career aboard Weston vessels. Beginning as a cabin boy on a Weston brig in 1821, Cushman served as a sailor aboard Weston's **Herald** and **Smyrna** in the late 1820s. He was mate of Weston's **Lagoda** in 1832 and **St. Lawrence** from 1833 to 1834. Weston then employed him as master of the ships **Undine** from 1842-1844 and **Mattakeesett** from 1844-1845. Cushman finished his career in 1860 as captain of the clipper **Kingfisher** for Augustus Hemenway of Boston. Photograph c. 1855.*

Five days later, "Sir…What arrangement might have been made at Philadelphia or Boston for the employment of the ship? I did not deem it necessary to remain at Richmond waiting the chance of your arrival, I recommend however, as also your instructions specify, that you proceed to Richmond and confirm with Mr. Palmer [Charles Palmer, Weston's broker in Richmond]."

The next day, "If you get a freight at Richmond [specifies rates]…you had better accept it, if not proceed direct to New Orleans and we think you might be able to obtain a tobacco freight without much detention but hope you will be able to obtain the above or higher rate in James River and should, if possible, get a direct freight to London."

After sending three more such letters over the next two weeks, and not hearing from Cushman, Weston grew impatient. "Capt Cushman, we are without any of your late favours and have nothing later than the 15 inst. But hope previous to this you have secured a freight and commenced loading. We have had nothing from Mr. Palmer later than yours of the 15th and wherefore we are entirely ignorant of your proceedings. Have been in daily expectation of hearing from you and wish you to keep us always advised of your prospects and progress if you make any. Therefore hope to hear of your engagement at Richmond."

Cushman, having difficulty securing a cargo at the challenging rates dictated by Weston, finally succeeded and sent word to Boston. Weston replied,

> *Sir, your favor of the 10th inst. has come to hand we are glad to hear you have succeeded in procuring a freight and hope you may meet with no detention in loading soon be off. We shall meet you with letters at your port of destination giving you our advice and on your arrival at Portsmouth you will advise Messrs Baring Bros & Company [Weston's primary supplier of credit and advice to his masters in England] of London of your port of discharge as I shall direct my letters to there to be forwarded to you…Your stay in James River has been Protracted much beyond our Expectations… Keep us advised at all times of your proceedings, keeping your expenses as low as possible and making all dispatch in your power.*[17]

Weston had 14 vessels in operation at this time. The firm's ability to supply such frequent and up-to-date advice to its masters is impressive. To Cushman, it must have been a bit exasperating.

Earlier, Cushman had learned an important lesson in dealing with King Caesar. Before commencing his first voyage as a master for Weston, he was cautioned by another master mariner to keep all correspondence with Weston concise. Upon reaching his first destination, Cushman anxiously penned a letter, evidently making an effort to compact his report into a single sentence, "We have arrived in England all right and are busy discharging the ship as quickly as possible and then shall load and sail at the first chance."[18]

King Caesar later told Cushman that it was the best letter he had ever received.

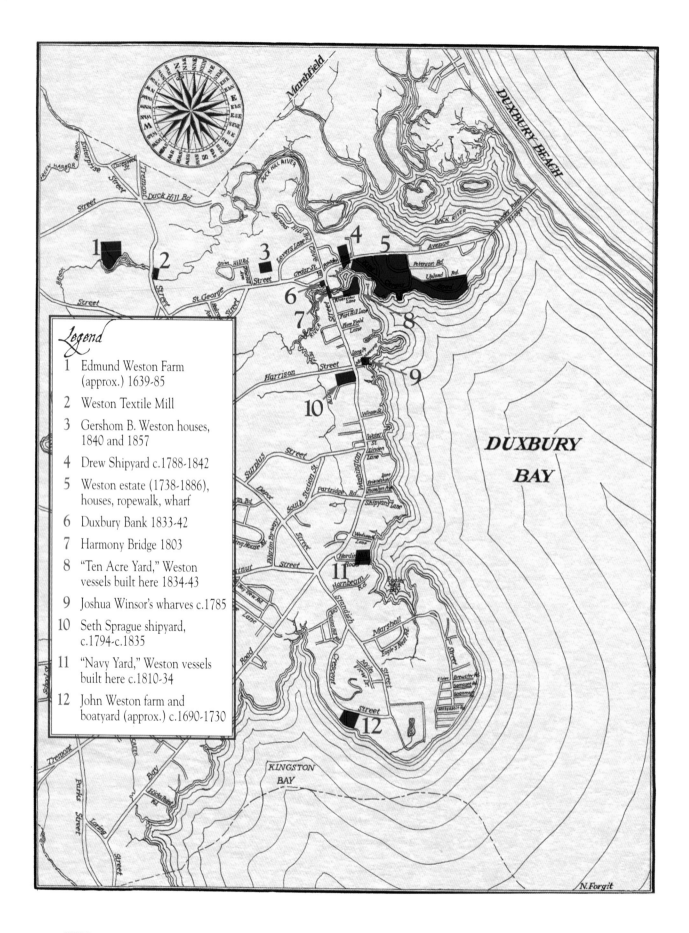

Legend

1 Edmund Weston Farm (approx.) 1639-85

2 Weston Textile Mill

3 Gershom B. Weston houses, 1840 and 1857

4 Drew Shipyard c.1788-1842

5 Weston estate (1738-1886), houses, ropewalk, wharf

6 Duxbury Bank 1833-42

7 Harmony Bridge 1803

8 "Ten Acre Yard," Weston vessels built here 1834-43

9 Joshua Winsor's wharves c.1785

10 Seth Sprague shipyard, c.1794-c.1835

11 "Navy Yard," Weston vessels built here c.1810-34

12 John Weston farm and boatyard (approx.) c.1690-1730

N. Forgit

CHAPTER SIX
The Late Fleet

Panic

In Natchez, Mississippi, on May 4, 1837, depositors rushed the banks.
The panic, soon felt throughout the west, tipped a national economy already weakened by land speculation. Five days later the panic reached New York, then Boston. Banks suspended payments and called in loans. Many businesses folded. The Panic of 1837 initiated a five-year depression, the worst in the nation's history up to that time.[1]

For many Duxbury shipbuilders, this depression signaled the end. The smaller shipyards were already in serious decline by the mid-1830s. Struggling with the challenges of building larger and larger vessels in a shallow bay, the shipbuilders could not cope with the added difficulties of lost capital and low freights in American ports. In March of 1838, King Caesar made a note in his book of the injunction placed on the Commercial Bank of Boston in which a few Duxbury merchants had invested. The bank later closed, taking its Duxbury investments with it. By 1840 only the Drew Family and King Caesar shipyards were still turning out vessels of any significant size.[2]

Subsequent to the panic, Weston received dismal letters from his captains in various ports telling of dull business and inability to secure decent freights. Weston's ship captains found themselves idle in ports. In 1842, Captain Josiah Knowles of Weston's ship *Minerva* wrote to another Weston captain, "Having a leisure moment, for in fact I have nothing but leisure moments as there is no business doing, I take the liberty of addressing you to inquire how freights are at James River…"[3]

Ships brokers, who were having a difficult time securing freights for ships entering their ports, felt the stresses as well. Captain David Cushman of Weston's ship

The Duxbury Bank (1833–1842)

The building on the left was originally built for the Duxbury Bank, which commenced business on September 30, 1833. It was built in the Greek Revival style, the first of several such public buildings in Duxbury whose striking architecture proclaimed a new height of prosperity for the town. Ezra Weston II was the bank's first President and the major shareholder. The other directors in 1833 were Charles J.F. Binney of Boston, Allen Danforth of Plymouth, and Peleg Jenkins of Scituate, as well as, from Duxbury, Charles Drew, Nathaniel Ford, Eleazar Harlow, George P. Richardson, Levi Sampson, William Sampson, Jacob Smith, and King Caesar's eldest son Gershom B. Weston who became President of the Bank in 1836. The establishment of a bank backed primarily by Weston is an important indication of his financial strength and success. Like Weston's firm, the Duxbury Bank weathered the Panic of 1837 when many did not. In fact, when director Jacob Smith resigned in the midst of the depression, he either felt compelled, or was requested, to print the following in the Old Colony Memorial in 1838, "Mr. Editor:

Permit me to say, through the medium of your paper, that I have resigned my office as Director in the Duxbury Bank; and that my resignation is not occasioned by any want of confidence in the soundness of the Bank. I know its present condition to be among the best in the Commonwealth."[4] Unfortunately, the bank could not be sustained

after the death of Ezra Weston II and was dissolved December 31, 1842. The building was later known as the Cable House, serving as the terminus of the trans-Atlantic telegraph line brought to Duxbury from France in 1869. The photograph was taken about 1890.

Two dollar bill issued by the Duxbury Bank

Undine, pressed by King Caesar to load his vessel and get on to London, received the following testy letter from Charles Palmer, the ships broker used by Weston in Richmond:

> *Sir, I must first thank you for your patience and confidence for your belief that I would do my best for you. I now have the pleasure to say I have engaged a full cargo for you to the continent…I expect to have business for [Capt. Byron] soon, also for several others now on the way. If a little patience more was exercised and masters of vessels would tell the truth and act like gentlemen, I could get along much better…[5]*

Writing later to Cushman, Weston acknowledged the difficulty his masters were having:

> *…From present appearances [I] do not think tis much of an object to wait [in port] long unless by so doing you see a good prospect of doing better, as lying by a month and then having to take what was first offered is bad. Yet tis also bad having to work for nothing and of the two evils must choose the least…. as every little helps these times.[6]*

For a time, the Drew family, Duxbury's second largest shipbuilding firm, was able to weather the storm with Weston, and they continued to build vessels well into the depression. However, in 1841 they suffered a misfortune. In May, their largest vessel, the ship *Susan Drew*, ran aground at Cape Ann. *The Old Colony Memorial* reported the incident:

> *The ship **Susan Drew**, which lately got ashore on Cape Ann, was hove out this morning at May's wharf. And any person, by examining her bottom, can bear testimony to the very superior manner in which she is put together and fastened. When ashore she struck heavily and it is surprising that she*

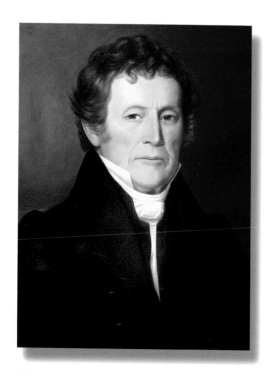

had not bilged and filled. It appears that the planks on her floor are much rubbed and chafed in many places and the keel is entirely gone to the garboard streak and broomed into the dead wood after, seven or eight inches! The ship must inevitably have filled, were it not for the superior and workmanlike manner in which the planks are fitted to the timbers. Notwithstanding the threshing she received, the pitch in her seams, even in the garboard, does not appear cracked, and the form of her bottom is not in the least degree out of line. It is truly gratifying to learn that so large a ship as the **Susan Drew**, over seven hundred tons, after stranding on a rough bottom, having on board more than a thousand tons of cargo, manifests by such unequivocal evidence, the faithful manner in which she was constructed, which must reflect great credit on the gentleman who built her and has always owned her, Charles Drew of Duxbury. We understand that this ship will be placed on the railway tomorrow morning, and in a few days will doubtless be completely repaired.[7]

Charles Drew I (1769-1858), painted by Cephas Thompson c. 1820. The Drew family of Duxbury, primarily under the leadership of Charles and brother Reuben Drew, mirrored the success of Ezra Weston II on a smaller scale, becoming the owners of the region's second largest merchant fleet.

This incident, heaped on top of other difficulties, was more than the Drews could manage. In December of 1842 they declared bankruptcy. King Caesar's sons purchased a good deal of the Drews' real estate at auction.[8]

With other shipyards in Duxbury closing and the situation grim, King Caesar devised a bold strategy. Although prices were falling and the promise of profitable trade looking worse with each month, he pushed his builder Samuel Cushing, in the midst of a depression, to build his largest vessels yet.

Hope

Spectators crowded both sides of the Bluefish River on May 20, 1841, their attention focused on the towering hull that sat on the river's south bank. She sat atop the ways, on the sloping bank of the tidal river, now reaching an astronomical high tide. The ship had been painted in the fashionable mode of the day, her hull jet black to the waterline, a bright white stripe around her waist painted intermittently with black squares that mimicked the gun ports of naval vessels. She dwarfed the shipyard buildings on either side of her.

On her deck, now crowded with men preparing for the launch and boys whose hard work or good luck had earned them a spot onboard, stood young John

*The **Hope** (880 tons), launched in Duxbury in 1841. With a colossal carrying capacity, the **Hope** broke records for shipping cotton under Captain Freeman Soule. After the Westons sold her in 1853, she made a voyage under new ownership to San Francisco and faded from the record.*

Photograph courtesy of the Duxbury Free Library.

Bradford. He was seventeen. Having been to sea twice he considered himself "pretty salt" and a step above the small lads on the deck with him. His first time to sea, back in 1839, had been on board Ezra Weston's ship *Oneco*. His father, Ephraim Bradford, hired by Ezra Weston I to run the Weston ropewalk, was still superintendent of that operation. John had labored many a day there under his father's direction. It was perhaps that distinction that earned him a spot on the deck of Ezra Weston's new ship during her launch.

Many of those assembled had seen vessels launched from Duxbury shores before, in the 1830s at a rate of roughly one every 45 days. But this one was different. The cause for true excitement and festivity was her size. A ship of 880 tons and 150 feet in length, she was larger even than the *Susan Drew* launched two years before from the Drew shipyard on the opposite bank of the river. At 700 tons the *Susan Drew* was the previous record holder. But here was Weston's new ship — a titan, the largest merchant vessel yet launched in New England.

Despite the economic downturn, Weston was pushing ahead on a grand scale, constructing eight vessels in the midst of the depression, many of them his largest and best. And now here sat the largest of them all. With other shipyards closing, Weston had built a giant. Surely there were some who shook their heads.

It may have seemed as if the old man had gone mad. He was indeed taking a tremendous risk, placing his faith almost exclusively in the ailing cotton market, its downturn currently one of the causes of the depression. His fleet, which had once been diverse in its cargo and ports of call, was increasingly focusing on a single trade route: shipping cotton from New Orleans to Liverpool. With the launching of his recent giants, bigger than any of Boston's freighters, Weston was poised to conduct the trade on the largest possible scale.[9]

The launching of this vessel, then, was not the result of madness or pride, but a daring optimism. It may well be the reason why King Caesar named his new ship the *Hope.*

John Bradford, standing on the deck of the *Hope,* was probably unaware of the master plan for the vessel. Like most, Bradford was caught up in the grandeur of the occasion. Later, he recalled that during ship launchings he was most enamored of the individual who had the privilege of standing on the bowsprit as the stern plowed into the water of the Bluefish River. That man, usually the master carpenter of the vessel, held a bottle of wine tied to the bow with a small lanyard. As the ship hit the water, steadying himself on his precarious position out on the bowsprit, he let loose the bottle. Back it swung against the bow and smashed, the master carpenter shouting words to the effect of, "Here's to the success of the good ship *Hope!*" And with that followed great cheers from the crowd.[10]

Once launched, the *Hope* must have been an odd sight wedged into the shallow inlet. The Bluefish at highest tide has a depth of about 12 feet. At about the same depth, the *Hope's* keel must have dug deep into the bottom as she slid off the ways. And as the tide went out, the *Hope* was left dry, sinking into mud of the exposed flats. Bradford wrote that it typically took three or four days to maneuver a vessel out of the river. In the case of the *Hope,* it took more than a week.

The Bluefish River. The grassy slope on the opposite bank is where Weston's Ten Acre Yard once stood and where the **Hope** was launched.

The first task was to position the ship so that she could be pulled out. This involved securing hawsers to each quarter of the vessel. At the next high tide, four teams of men on the banks of the river would heave and pull until she was faced downriver. John Bradford was on one of those teams. Next came the difficult task of hauling her around the curve of the river, again, conducted by rope teams from the shore. Often empty casks were lashed around large vessels to aid in floating them. Even with that assistance, there would only be a short time during each high tide when the *Hope* could be moved.[11]

Once out into the harbor, Weston vessels were typically brought to his wharf near the mouth of the river to be fitted out with upper masts, rigging, and sails. Due to her size, this was impossible for the *Hope*. Instead, she was brought out to the Cowyard, an area of deep water in Duxbury Bay west of Clark's Island. There, the ship was fitted out by a crew who lived on board during the three-month operation. John Bradford was among them. He must have proven himself a capable hand. When the *Hope* sailed for Boston, Bradford was permitted to stay on board for her first run.

The *Hope* remained in Boston for nearly two months as she was provisioned and a freight of sundries for New Orleans was procured. She left Boston on October 15, 1841, and after a swift trip of 15 days went up river to New Orleans, there to begin a remarkable career bringing financial success to the firm E. Weston & Son.

For John Bradford it was just the beginning of a long association with the *Hope*. Perhaps he dared to dream it as a seventeen-year-old helping to rig Ezra Weston's finest ship. In nine years he would be her master.

Voyages & Cargo

Examining data available from the firm's records of the 1830s and 1840s, it is clear that cotton shipped from New Orleans, and to a lesser extent from Charleston and Mobile, was the most profitable and significant activity of the fleet. To better understand the full scope of the fleet's voyages, the chart on the next page summarizes the number of arrivals of Weston vessels in their top 15 ports of call (excluding their home port of Boston). These ports account for 67% of the fleet's activity. The remaining 33% percent of voyages (not reflected in the chart below) were to diverse locations in the Atlantic and Mediterranean, many of which were visited only once and not part of any specific trade pattern.

While providing a good idea of where King Caesar's vessels were sent during the late era of the firm, this analysis does not reveal the particular patterns of trade in which he was involved (except, perhaps, the obvious emphasis on New Orleans cotton). For instance, New York was clearly an important port, but why? When Weston captains arrived there were they outward bound to Europe or returning home? In order to explore Weston's trade patterns, it is important to first examine the departure of his vessels from Boston. Determining where they went first, and where they proceeded next, reveals that King Caesar was involved in at least four other important markets besides cotton.

Leaving Boston, one third of Weston's fleet was bound for other American ports, and half of these trips were to New Orleans or Mobile for cotton. Leaving aside,

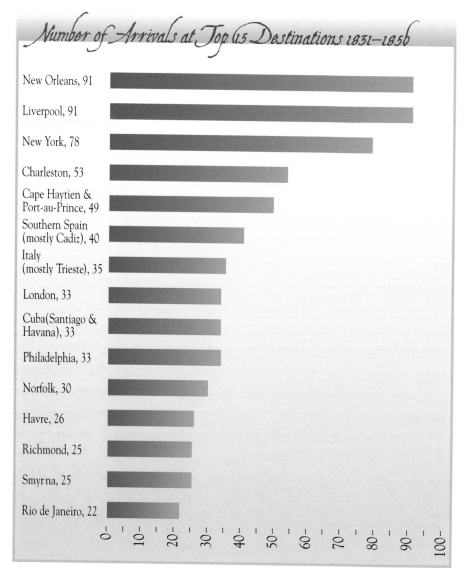

Number of Arrivals at Top 45 Destinations 1831–1856

New Orleans, 91	
Liverpool, 91	
New York, 78	
Charleston, 53	
Cape Haytien & Port-au-Prince, 49	
Southern Spain (mostly Cadiz), 40	
Italy (mostly Trieste), 35	
London, 33	
Cuba(Santiago & Havana), 33	
Philadelphia, 33	
Norfolk, 30	
Havre, 26	
Richmond, 25	
Smyrna, 25	
Rio de Janeiro, 22	

for the moment, Weston's vessels involved in the New Orleans cotton trade, let us first examine his vessels that went to other southern ports, primarily Charleston and Richmond.

In Charleston, the vessels picked up rice or cotton and brought them to ports in northern Europe, mostly London. In Richmond Weston's trade was primarily tobacco. From Richmond most of the vessels also went on to London. After arriving in London, 56% of the vessels returned to Boston and New York carrying passengers from England. In fact, a plurality of the arrivals of Weston vessels in New York had to do with this passenger trade from London and Liverpool. The rest returned to Charleston to make another run of rice and cotton.

Weston's ship *Minerva*, for example, was involved in the rice trade for much of her career. In December 1838, Captain Alexander Wadsworth of Duxbury stepped aboard the *Minerva* at Charleston, relieving Zaddock Bradford who had served as the ship's master for the previous year. Most changes in masters took place in Boston, however it was not uncommon for King Caesar to send a captain down to a southern port to take charge of a vessel if he felt it necessary. Wadsworth, who had already distinguished himself as a master mariner sailing vessels owned by his grandfather Seth Sprague, was sailing for King Caesar for the first time.

In Charleston, Wadsworth proceeded to load the vessel with 17,000 pounds of rice. He departed for London on December 20 and arrived six weeks later, earning a modest £644 on the cargo, a typical profit for the *Minerva*. Then it was back to Charleston for another run. Wadsworth arrived a month later and loaded 18,000 pounds of rice for the return trip to London. From London he tried something

Vessels Departing Boston, 1831–1856

Destination	Number of Departures	Percentage of Total Departures
Southern United States	84	27%
New Orleans	34	
Charleston	14	
Norfolk	13	
Richmond	13	
Mobile	5	
Fredericksburg	3	
Savannah	2	
Haiti and Cuba	68	22%
Cape Haytien, Haiti	18	
Port au Prince, Haiti	15	
Santiago du Cuba, Cuba	9	
Havana, Cuba	9	
Aux Cayes, Haiti	8	
Jeremie, Haiti	7	
Gonaives, Haiti	2	
Western Mediterranean	36	12%
Marseilles, France	9	
Malta	8	
Trieste, Italy	8	
Gibraltar, Spain	5	
Malaga, Spain	3	
Genoa, Italy	1	
Leghorn, Italy	1	
Venice, Italy	1	
South America	20	6%
Rio de Janeiro, Brazil	10	
Pernambuco, Brazil	5	
Monte Video, Trinidad	4	
Buenos Aires, Argentina	1	
Near East	14	5%
Smyrna, Turkey	13	
Constantinople, Turkey	1	
Northern United States	14	5%
New York	7	
Philadelphia	7	
Northern Europe	17	5%
Cronstadt, Russia	6	
London, England	4	
Antwerp, Belgium	3	
Bremen, Germany	2	
Amsterdam, Netherlands	1	
Havre, France	1	
Miscellaneous	57	18%

different, setting sail for Cadiz on July 29, 1839 and arriving two weeks later. After loading an unspecified cargo in Cadiz, probably fruit, he set sail for Duxbury. It was a tour of nearly a year. Wadsworth would complete two more such tours aboard the *Minerva*.

Pursuing a different trade route, about 22% of Weston's vessels left Boston heading for Cuba and present-day Haiti. This trade focused primarily on coffee, but also included sugar, timber, flour, and hides. Unlike the ships employed in Weston's other areas of trade, these vessels almost always (85% of the time) turned about and brought their coffee directly back to Boston rather than proceeding to another port. This form of trade was less significant in the 1830s but became more important to the Weston firm over time, with a marked increase in voyages to Haiti in the late 1840s and early 1850s.

A typical ship involved in this trade was the brig *Trenton*, launched in 1836. On December 18, 1836, she departed Boston for Havana with Captain Lewis Peterson commanding. A relatively new captain for King Caesar, Peterson would eventually serve as master of seven of his vessels. This was his second command, having just come from the *Levant*. On reaching Havana, Captain Peterson loaded a cargo of sugar and molasses. This was brought back to

Boston in a fast trip of two weeks. Peterson repeated this run twice over the next year after which the *Trenton* moved on for a few runs in the Mediterranean trade.

The western Mediterranean was another significant trade route for the Weston fleet, representing about 12% of Boston departures. Weston traded in a variety of ports, most significantly Marseilles, Malta, and Trieste on the Adriatic. A typical trip for these vessels was to make two stops in any of the aforementioned ports and then return to Boston or sometimes New York. The brig *Trenton*, for example, returned to New York from Messina, Sicily, in 1840 with 3,300 boxes of oranges and lemons worth $1,400. The vessels involved in the Mediterranean trade were often the same as those in the sugar and coffee trade. These mid-sized brigs of the Weston fleet typically spent one year running coffee from Brazil or Haiti, then the next year in the Mediterranean.

About 6% of Weston's vessels left Boston bound for South America. Most of these headed for Rio de Janeiro, again trading primarily in coffee. Unlike their counterparts who brought West Indies coffee back to Boston, shippers of Brazilian coffee had a broader market. The coffee Weston shipped from Rio de Janeiro was split in even thirds, one part to Boston, one to New York, and another to New Orleans. Again, the firm's involvement in the coffee market was mostly a phenomenon of the 1840s. The brig *Lion* was involved in this trade intermittently during the 1840s and 1850s. A trip from Boston to Rio de Janeiro and back took about 5 months, usually carrying roughly 3,000 bags of coffee.

Captain Lewis Peterson (1804-1863) served a total of 7 years at sea for King Caesar. Peterson's association with the Weston fleet began in 1833 and ended in 1849. During that time he was master of 7 Weston vessels.

Weston traded far less in Smyrna (now Izmir), Turkey, but that business was economically and politically significant nonetheless. During the 1820s, Weston was one of the American pioneers in this route. Of the 21 arrivals of American vessels in Smyrna in 1825, three were Weston vessels. He maintained an important stake in the trade through the 1840s.[12]

A page from "E. Weston's Vessel Memorandum Book" kept by Alden B. Weston. This meticulous record book provides the majority of surviving information on the voyages of the Weston fleet from 1830 to 1857.

The near eastern trade had always been a dangerous one due to pirates from the Barbary Coast and Aleppo prowling the Mediterranean. Few American merchant houses dared to engage in it. Those that did were almost exclusively from Boston, Duxbury, and Salem (63%, 10%, and 6%, respectively, from 1823 to 1839). Initially attracted by exotic cargos of figs and raisins, Massachusetts merchants quickly tapped into a more profitable trade—opium. Turkish opium fueled the addiction of the Chinese populace with colossal and well-known political

Launched in Duxbury in 1829, Weston's brig **Neptune** *was built by Samuel Hall. She was used mostly in the Mediterranean trade to Marseilles, Messina, Trieste, and other ports. She is shown here rigged as a brigantine, probably under later ownership. Weston sold her to Robert Brookhouse of Salem on January 19, 1841. Original watercolor by Francois Joseph Frederic Roux.*

Photograph courtesy of the Peabody Essex Museum.

ramifications, and Chinese resistance to the trade eventually resulted in two Opium Wars in 1839-1842 and 1856-1860. Opium was typically shipped from Smyrna then transferred in Boston to vessels bound for China. The Boston merchant house of J. & T. H. Perkins & Co. held a virtual monopoly in this trade.[13]

Most of Weston's vessels bound for Smyrna in the 1830s and 1840s sailed from Boston. Once there, they loaded opium, wool, figs, and raisins and set sail for Massachusetts. It is not clear whether Weston vessels transferred their opium cargo to other ships in Gibraltar (as many involved in the trade did) or on the wharves of Boston. Either way, Weston was never involved in bringing opium directly to China.

Although the opium trade represented a small percentage of the firm's overall activity (5% of voyages), it must have been profitable and Weston evidently placed some importance on it. Two of his brigs were named the *Smyrna* and two the *Levant* (a traditional term for the Near East). During one voyage, a Weston vessel garnered its owner an interesting claim to fame. In 1830 the brig *Smyrna*, with Seth F. Sprague commanding, was granted permission by the Sultan of Turkey to enter the Black Sea. According to the clearance documents issued to

Sprague by the Sultan and the American consul, the *Smyrna* was the first American vessel to enter that sea.

In America the opium trade was a politically charged issue because of its adverse effects on the Chinese. There were also fears that merchants might one day begin widespread distribution of the drug in America or England resulting in rampant addiction. There is no evidence, however, that Weston himself was ever subjected to criticism for his involvement in this legal but unpopular trade.

As Weston vessels returned to the United States from these various trade routes, most of them (80%) concluded their voyages in Boston. The remaining 20% stopped in New York to unload their passengers, coffee, fruit, and other cargoes. Thus, most of the fleet's arrivals in New York were due to the use of that port as a terminus for their trade. After unloading, it was home to Massachusetts to begin again.[14]

*Clearance issued by the Sultan of Turkey to Captain Seth F. Sprague of Weston's brig Smyrna in 1830. The document proclaims that the **Smyrna** is "the first American vessel to enter the Black Sea."*

Photograph courtesy of the Duxbury Free Library.

Cotton

Captain Freeman Soule commanded the *Hope* as she embarked on her first voyage in October of 1841. Soule was a man with a goal. He was bringing Weston's largest cotton freighter into New Orleans for the first time. And he would leave the city having broken a record.

Reaching the Mississippi, the *Hope* was towed by steamboat up the river to the city. Later, another master of the *Hope*, Captain John Bradford, would bring his young daughter on such a voyage aboard a different ship. She described the experience of coming into New Orleans with a recollection of her childhood enthusiasm:

> How exciting it always was to be towed up the Mississippi from the bar in the South West Pass. "Cream and molasses," suggesting Grandma's thick cream and the New Orleans molasses that was used on the table in those days, was what my mother and I called the muddy waters swirling in the wake. On shore were attractive plantation houses nestled in orange groves while on the wide, level plain about five miles below the city I was told the Battle of New Orleans had been fought in 1815. That was forgotten at the sight of the forest of masts edging the levee as we approached the business part of the city. Warping the ship into her berth opposite Post 61 was a breathless undertaking...[15]

When Captain Soule first docked the *Hope* in New Orleans in 1841, the ship attracted a great deal of attention due to its size. Now came the arduous process of loading cotton. Specialized stevedores, sometimes known as "cotton jammers," were engaged who, using screws and presses, packed the massive cotton bales into the ship's hold. Particularly adept stevedores, out of sheer strength and determination, could increase the ship's cargo capacity by 15%. Sometimes bales were packed so tightly that the seams of the vessel split apart. [16]

When the *Hope* was fully loaded, she shipped 3,132 bales of cotton worth roughly £2,382. It was the largest cargo of cotton that had ever been shipped out of the city. When the ship arrived in Liverpool on January 1, 1842, 45 days after leaving New Orleans, she created another stir due to the size of the cargo. The *Hope* was just about on par with the largest vessels owned by New York merchants of the day. By 1845, she was still among the top 1% of Liverpool cotton freighters, although by that time a number of New York vessels had been built that were over

The last of the Weston firm's great cotton freighters, the Manteo was also the last vessel launched from the Weston Ten Acre Shipyard in 1843.

Collection of Grace Weston-Kynoch and Bradford Weston III

1,000 tons. Still, the *Hope* consistently shipped more cotton in a single voyage than any of the other vessels bringing cotton into Liverpool. In the latter half of 1845, the size of the average cargo of cotton was about 1,300 bales. The *Hope* usually shipped 3,000. Perhaps it was something about the design of her cargo hold. Perhaps it was Captain Soule's determination to pack the largest possible cargo into the ship. Either way, the *Hope* was clearly a pioneering and hugely successful part of King Caesar's strategy to enter the cotton trade in a significant way. [17]

King Caesar's gravitation toward the cotton trade began in the mid 1830s. At that time some of his smaller vessels, the *Margaret* and the *Undine* among them, dipped into the trade by bringing small cargoes of cotton from Charleston and Mobile to Marseilles and Amsterdam. Soon, his biggest vessel at the time, the *Mattakeesett*, was making profitable runs from New Orleans to Liverpool (the largest market for American cotton). Early on, King Caesar's masters experimented with different ports, on four occasions conveying cotton from the south to Boston and Portsmouth, New Hampshire. In this fashion, Weston vessels acted as "middle men," shipping cotton to merchants in those New England cities who then shipped it on to England. Such a supply line was ideal for the Boston merchants who were spared the inconvenience of having to send ships to New Orleans to get their cotton. For Weston, however, trading in this capacity did not enable him to capitalize on the high rates being paid in England and France. His experimentation with this part of the cotton trade was fleeting. To make a decent profit, it was clear that he had to ship cotton direct to the markets willing to pay the most.

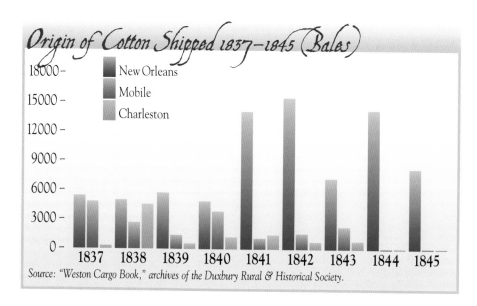

A portion of the cargo list from the **Hope**'s first voyage from New Orleans on November 17, 1841, from Alden B. Weston's cargo book kept from 1836 to 1846.

The chart below shows the evolution of Weston's reliance on New Orleans cotton. Initially, his sources were fairly evenly divided between Charleston, Mobile, and New Orleans. With the launching of the firm's great cotton freighters (the *Oneco*, the *Hope*, and the *Manteo*) beginning in 1839, the scope of his trade narrows, eventually focusing almost exclusively on the supply from New Orleans. Leaving the Mississippi River, 79% of this cotton was bound for Liverpool, 14% for Havre, France, 2% to London and 2% to Boston.

Origin of Cotton Shipped 1837–1845 (Bales)

- New Orleans
- Mobile
- Charleston

Source: "Weston Cargo Book," archives of the Duxbury Rural & Historical Society.

With its massive warehouses and huge steam-powered mills, Liverpool was rapidly becoming the world's capitol of textile production. One of the agents for the Weston firm, William V. Kent of Duxbury, recorded his impressions of Liverpool during a trip there on Weston business. The responsibilities of an "agent" varied broadly, from acting as supercargo to simply carrying letters. On this trip Kent was supercargo of a vessel that did not belong to the Weston firm, but King Caesar's sons had given him a short list of tasks to complete in Liverpool. Most importantly, he was to deliver correspondence to agents of Baring Brothers & Co., the Westons' primary suppliers of credit.

Kent's voyage had been difficult. As a supercargo, he had spent plenty of time aboard ship, however, he did not seem to grow accustomed to the experience. During a storm, which the captain noted was the worst he'd ever seen, Kent wrote, "I am truly sick of a winter's ocean. I yearn for a fair wind and a smooth sea…Give me the top point of Mount Washington in a hail storm rather than what I have experienced."[18]

Arriving in Liverpool, Kent was greatly impressed by the scale of the city. "The warehouses for cotton are particularly well constructed, heavy massive walls of brick and great facilities for taking in and pulling out merchandise. They are usually eight stories high and are located parallel with the river and docks. The dray horses are very large and carry tremendous loads. I saw one this morning with 75 barrels of flour on it, another with 60 bales of cotton."[19]

The city had its negative aspects as well. "Poverty causes us to do many things which if in prosperity we should shudder at," Kent wrote, noting that the destitute filled the streets by the "thousands." Coming home from a play and "bestowing a few half pence on some miserable objects, apparently for charity, I wended my way home at 11½ o'clock and went to bed reflecting how little we know in America of suffering and misery."

Fulfilling his obligations to the Westons, Kent delivered his correspondence. His brief mention of the transaction gives some indication of the challenges faced by merchants from Duxbury who operated on the world stage.

> I called on Mr. Gain of the firm Baring Brothers & Co. who politely gave me an invitation to dine with him on Monday evening next at 6 pm. He observes he has made up only a small party with the only flattering remark that he loves to entertain his American friends…No doubt they should look on me as an unsophisticated 'Jonathan,' but I may by chance get along without any discredit to myself or nation.[20]

In the latter half of 1842, the Weston firm shipped about 1.5% of all the cotton that entered Liverpool. Indications are that the firm continued to ship cotton at this rate throughout the 1840s. While this may seem like a small amount, it places them as significant players in a large world market. The firm would continue its involvement in the cotton trade until the Weston fleet began to dwindle in 1853.[21]

It appears King Caesar's risky scheme of constructing a fleet of cotton freighters was indeed successful in boosting the profits of the firm, although perhaps not to the extent he expected given the decreasing prices of cotton. The years 1838 and 1840 saw rather high prices for cotton in Liverpool. This upward trend must have been a factor in Weston's decision to focus on the cotton trade. In 1837, although shipping relatively small amounts of cotton, Weston vessels grossed roughly £12,000 on the cargo. Six years later, with large freighters in operation, the firm shipped nearly twice as much. Had rates remained the same, their profit should have increased 100%. However, because prices fell and stabilized, the firm's income only increased 66%. Had King Caesar lived to see this sluggish trend of the late 1840s, he probably would have found the results disappointing. However, the strategy was successful enough to allow his sons to continue the operation for 15 years after King Caesar's death.

There was a flipside to the cotton trade: immigration. With their large cargo holds, Weston's cotton freighters could easily be converted into immigrant ships through the installation of bunks and a very few other amenities. After completing her first voyage from New Orleans, the *Hope* took on in Liverpool a total of 270 passengers bound for New Orleans. The group was part of a large emigration of Mormons from England to the community of Nauvoo, Illinois. Departing in February 1842, the Mormons paid £3 to £4 each for passage, including provisions. "Passengers find their own bedding and cooking utensils, and all the luggage goes free," observed the *Millennial Star*, the Mormon paper reporting on the *Hope's* departure in 1842.[22]

Alden Weston apparently did not keep track of passengers, so it is difficult to determine the full extent of the Westons' role in immigration. After King Caesar's death, Liverpool became one of the primary points of departure for Irish immigrants fleeing their country during the Potato Famine. New Orleans was an attractive destination for these immigrants due to the availability of land in the American West. With Weston freighters passing so regularly (about once every four months) between those two ports at the height of the famine, the firm's involvement in immigration to New Orleans must have been considerable.

Alden B. Weston's epitaph to the ship **Hope** *on her sale in 1853 as recorded in the Vessel Memorandum Book.*

After shipping about 29,000,000 pounds of cotton and an unknown number of immigrants (possibly as many as 5,000) across the Atlantic over 12 years, the *Hope* finally came to dock in New York on November 9, 1853. She was sold three weeks later. The vessel had served the firm well and lived up to King Caesar's daring expectations. Alden Weston, who rarely recorded anything but statistics in his memoranda books, wrote an uncharacteristic remark next to the notation of the Hope's sale. "Good luck attend her."[23]

Oneco

Launched in 1839, the *Oneco* was the second largest vessel built by the Weston firm. At 650 tons, she was 147 feet long and 31 feet in breadth. She would prove to be one of Weston's most dependable cotton freighters, and a good example of how King Caesar realized his aspiration to build the largest and the best fleet of ships in Massachusetts.

It has already been noted that Weston's vessels kept, with very few exceptions, to the Atlantic and Mediterranean, having no interest in the Asian markets that were popular sources of revenue during his time. His sons, however, did make an experimental effort in the direction of the Far East. At the height of the California gold rush in 1849, E. Weston & Sons sent the *Oneco* to San Francisco and then on to Sydney, Hong Kong, and Calcutta. In doing so, they exposed the ship to a new variety of dangers to which Weston's Duxbury sailors were not accustomed. In the course of this voyage, the *Oneco* became the only Weston vessel to circumnavigate the globe.

*Launched in Duxbury in 1839, at a massive 640 tons, the **Oneco** represents Weston's commitment to building large freighters for transporting cotton.*

The ship left Boston on November 26, 1849, "loaded down with gold hunters," according to one of her crew. To accommodate the passengers, her deck-houses were fitted out with comfortable quarters, far better than those in which the 22 or so crewmen slept. She was under the direction of Captain Joshua Drew. He had served as master of the *Oneco* for the better part of ten years. Running her in the cotton trade during the 1840s, Drew and his crew were usually away from Duxbury for a bit more than a year at a time, spending 13 months making two round trips across the Atlantic, then returning for about a month at home. This was typical for a Weston cotton vessel. This voyage, however, would keep Drew away from home for far longer.

The *Oneco* arrived in San Francisco from Boston on June 23, 1850, after a voyage of 209 days. The prestige of Weston's vessels lay in their cargo capacity and certainly not their speed. How astounded the crew must have been when the extreme clipper ship *Sea Witch* arrived in San Francisco a month after them, having made the trip from New York in a record 97 days.

On her way to Hong Kong, the *Oneco* proceeded first to Sydney. Here she picked up a new crew member, an American sailor named Bradley Osbon. Twenty-two at the time, Osbon would go on to become an accomplished naval officer, serving

*An account of the last voyages of the **Oneco** from Alden B. Weston's "Vessel Memorandum Book."*

under Admiral Farragut during the Civil War. When he boarded the *Oneco*, however, his lofty ambitions went no further than the occupation of the fine quarters that had been set up for the gold hunters, now taken over by the crew. "I was the only sailor on her not born on Cape Cod," Osbon later observed.

In his memoirs, published in 1906, Osbon tells of the dangers encountered by the *Oneco* in her tour around the Pacific. The trouble began when the ship, bound for Manila, stopped for wood and water at the Ladrone Islands. Captain Drew, concerned about the number of natives who crowded about his vessel in canoes, wisely did not allow his crew to go ashore. Instead, he kept them busy painting the ship inside and out. Osbon wrote,

> On the morning we were to sail a large collection of [natives in canoes] appeared, the men all armed. We made up our minds that we were to have trouble and hastily shotted our guns, loaded our pistols and sharpened our cutlasses…Then we began to heave the anchor, but by the time it was fairly clear of the ground, the fellows opened fire on us with arrows and stones, which we returned with bullets, killing a great number. They came on for a time, yelling, and firing with bows and slings, but our return fire was more than they could stand and they dropped back out of range, though still following.[24]

The captain had brought a native on board to act as pilot, guiding the ship out of the harbor with all possible speed. When the attack began, the crew suspected that the pilot's plan was to wreck the vessel on shoals, allowing the natives to overtake the ship. The third mate dragged the poor man aloft, holding a pistol to him and saying that if the ship ran aground he would be shot. The pilot guided them out and was rewarded with some tobacco and calico, then told to swim for shore.

The *Oneco* then proceeded towards Hong Kong:

> We were about two days from our destination when we ran into a thick fog, where we clewed up our topgallant sail, hauled up the mainsail, lowered

the topsails on the cap and jogged along, waiting for the fog to lift. We had
been in the fog but for two or three hours when a large junk suddenly loomed
up on our port bow. Our Captain…took one look at her and said,
"My God! Here's an infernal Chinese pirate junk! Make all sail, quick!"
We did not need that order. Almost as soon as I can tell it we had the sails
up and drawing, but not quick enough to escape the junk, which bore
down under full head, her decks crowded with men, her grappling irons on
a long pole ready to hook onto our chains.[25]

Preparations had been made for an encounter such as this. The *Oneco* mounted
an impressive array of armament for her Pacific voyage, with four guns on each
broadside, two swivel guns astern, and a large supply of small arms. It is unlikely
that the ship carried so much firepower during her long service in the Atlantic
where the danger of privateer attacks was, for the most part, a thing of the past.
Osbon spoke highly of Captain Drew's leadership during the encounter, writing
that he was "on old East India and China Trader" who responded with great
courage in beating back a foe he had encountered before. In fact, Drew was an
Atlantic cotton trader. If he had been to the Pacific before, it was long before
and not on board the *Oneco*. It must have been a shock for these Duxbury men,
accustomed to calm runs from New Orleans to Liverpool, to find themselves
suddenly at war in the Pacific. Still, they rose to the occasion bravely. Osbon
described what happened next:

We had not fired a gun before his grappling irons were in our chains. But in
this moment we let go a broadside of our four port guns, which must have
disabled the men in charge of the grappling line…We now shifted some
of our guns from the starboard side, and our third mate, Mr. Nye, a very
strong man, assisted by a couple of sailors, carried one of them to the top of
the deck house where there was a better range, while some of the men went
up into the mizzentop with muskets and opened fire from there. The pirates…
at last opened with what was apparently a twelve pound pivot gun, doing
little damage. Their chief effort was to haul up along side us so that they
could board us, but we kept up such a hot fire that they failed to succeed in
this plan.… At the end of about three quarters of an hour an accidental
shot from somewhere cut the grappling line and we were free. But our
Captain's blood was up now and we headed for her and gave her a broadside
that cut away her foremast and made havoc among her men.[26]

After delivering this crippling blow, Drew wisely decided that it was time to make
for Hong Kong. Upon arrival, he notified the captain of an English sloop-of-war
in the harbor of their encounter with the pirates. The warship immediately sailed,

found the disabled Chinese vessel, and took the survivors prisoner. All were executed in Hong Kong.

While the *Oneco* proceeded to bring passengers on board, Osbon decided he had developed a taste for fighting pirates. He disembarked and enlisted with "a flotilla that made pirate hunting its daily occupation."

More than 50 years later, a Duxbury resident read Osbon's memoirs and, finding a photograph of a portrait of the *Oneco*, mailed it to him. Osbon, who was approaching 90 at the time, wrote back, "You cannot imagine what a treat, what a treasure you have sent me...I have been up aloft on the picture and furled the sky sail and then the royal and then out and stowed the flying jib and then went aft and took a trick at the wheel....Oh, the happy stirring days I spent on boards that good ship with that good skipper, for I was very fond of him and regretted leaving him."[27]

Joshua Drew sailed the *Oneco* back to San Francisco, made one more run across the Pacific, and then sailed to Calcutta. After making repairs and taking on a cargo, the ship set out for home, rounding the Cape of Good Hope on June 16, 1852. On August 20, the crew spotted the lighthouse at Chatham, Massachusetts. That afternoon, for the first time in three years, the *Oneco* tied up outside the counting rooms of E. Weston & Sons on Boston's Commercial Wharf.

Vulture

By 1841, King Caesar's health was beginning to fail. He was still the head of the firm's affairs, but at this point he probably relied greatly on his son Alden to manage what he couldn't. The cause of his illness is unknown. The decline was slow.

In 1842, the operation of Weston's fleet was in full swing. Still defying the economic depression, around January of that year he ordered Samuel Cushing to begin the construction of a small brig. He then had 14 vessels afloat, a fleet totaling 4,300 tons. The firm's trade in cotton had yet to reach its peak. King Caesar could be satisfied in the fact that there were no indications that the firm was slowing.

When the new brig was launched on April 2, 1842, it was the last Weston would see leave the ways in his yard. He died four months later on August 15, 1842. The cause of death noted in his record was "marasmus," a medical term for starvation. The circumstances leading to this are a mystery, but it seems it must have been the final result of some debilitating illness. *The Old Colony Memorial* printed a short obituary:[28]

> *In Duxbury, the 15 inst., Ezra Weston, Esqr. 70. Mr. Weston was long known as one of the largest ship owners in Massachusetts. He was an active and successful merchant, indeed he was industrious, and so devoted to business as to probably impair his health, which for two years has been very feeble. But he was not grasping nor avaricious, and no one could accuse him of dishonesty or oppression, or over-reaching his business. He usually employed a great number of mechanics, who always bore witness to his integrity and kindness.*[29]

King Caesar's sons, Gershom, Alden and Ezra IV were left to administer the firm's affairs. Alden, having so long managed the counting house and the firm's records, was up to the challenge. With so many vessels in operation, there was probably little doubt as to whether or not to keep the firm in business. If there was any discussion, it was decided quickly. Less than two weeks after their father's death, the sons posted the following notice in the *Old Colony Memorial*.

> *Notice: The copartnership of E. Weston & Sons having been dissolved on the 15th inst. in consequence of the decease of the senior partner, the surviving partners give notice that the affairs of the late firm will be settled by them and that they will continue business in copartnership under the same style as before. GB Weston, AB Weston, E Weston*[30]

As a weakened Ezra Weston II watched that brig under construction in 1842, he gave her a name laced with morose irony and we are left to wonder if he did so with a sense of his own mortality in mind. He called her the *Vulture*.

Weston with Dog, 1840s

The images shown here represent two of Duxbury's earliest photographs and also a perplexing mystery.

The images are daguerreotypes, one of the first forms of photography, a process perfected by Louis J. M. Daguerre in France in 1839. Just months after he made the invention public, lectures on the process were being given throughout Europe and the United States. By 1840, riding a wave of fascination, numerous photographic studios began to appear in American cities. The photographs shown here are consistent with the earliest daguerreotypes produced in the United States.

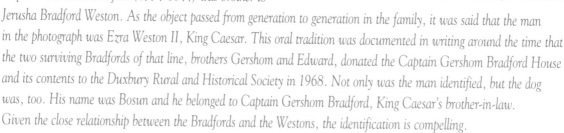

The top photograph belonged to the Bradford family of Duxbury. Captain Gershom Bradford (1774-1844) was brother to Jerusha Bradford Weston. As the object passed from generation to generation in the family, it was said that the man in the photograph was Ezra Weston II, King Caesar. This oral tradition was documented in writing around the time that the two surviving Bradfords of that line, brothers Gershom and Edward, donated the Captain Gershom Bradford House and its contents to the Duxbury Rural and Historical Society in 1968. Not only was the man identified, but the dog was, too. His name was Bosun and he belonged to Captain Gershom Bradford, King Caesar's brother-in-law. Given the close relationship between the Bradfords and the Westons, the identification is compelling.

When the Duxbury Rural and Historical Society recently publicized the interesting photograph, a descendant of Ezra Weston II, living in greater San Francisco, read about it on the Society's website. He immediately sent to the Society a copy of the lower photograph, which had been in his family for generations but was unidentified. Clearly, the two photographs were taken on the same occasion. That one of these photographs descended in the Weston family is strong evidence that the subject is indeed a Weston. But which one?

Identifying the age of the subject is difficult given the lack of clarity, however it seems that he is younger than the 67-69 years of age that Ezra II would have been if the photograph was taken during the last years of his life (he died in 1842). There is the possibility that the subject is Ezra Weston IV, King Caesar's youngest son. However, comparing the photographs with the only photographic portrait of Ezra IV reveals inconsistencies.

Leaving aside the identity of the man, the location is perhaps most significant. The setting is almost certainly the shoreline of Duxbury, possibly at or near the Weston Ten Acre Yard on the Bluefish River. In the background of the upper photograph can be seen scaffolding of the type erected for the construction of a vessel. Only two other photographs (two angles of the same vessel under construction in 1869) are known to exist of a working Duxbury shipyard.

Here, then, are two intriguing and exceedingly rare images of a member of the Weston family in a working Duxbury shipyard. Bottom photograph courtesy of William Bradford Drury.

Chapter Seven

The Sons

Selling Ships

There would be no King Caesar III.

Social and political conditions in Duxbury had changed by the time of King Caesar's death. With the shipbuilding industry in decline, residents of Duxbury had little interest in "crowning" another Weston. Also, with three sons now inheriting the firm, there was no single monarch to lay claim to the title. Having spent 30 years or so handling the firm's accounts, Alden may have been the son most worthy of the title. He was, however, extremely conservative and retiring and would have shunned such a label.

The eldest son, Gershom, probably would have enjoyed the title. A vibrant character, he did not shy away from expansive displays of his status. He enjoyed a successful political career and energetically attempted to mold Duxbury's political environment just as his father had controlled its economy a generation before. Gershom had a certain following, but his radical support of the antislavery and temperance movements made him the target of much controversy. Indeed, the disapproval leveled at him is a telling symptom of the changes in Duxbury's social and economic condition.

King Caesar's death signaled the end of shipbuilding for the Weston firm. Samuel Cushing built just one more vessel for the Westons in 1843. The *Manteo*, the firm's third largest ship at 599 tons, was the last of the Westons' great cotton freighters. After that, the sons closed the Ten Acre Shipyard on the Bluefish River. Three more small schooners were acquired 1843-1846 for coastal trade, but these were probably not built in the Weston yard.

The sons' decision to stop building ships in Duxbury was a dramatic one. There are some indications that Gershom desired to build clipper ships in Boston, so the

Brig Lion of Duxbury L. Peterson Comander Entering Smyrna. 3° aprile 1840.

Launched in Duxbury in 1839, the brig **Lion** had the distinction of being the last vessel sold by the Weston firm (in February of 1857). Serving the Westons for 18 years, she made 75 voyages under their ownership.

Photograph courtesy of Mr. and Mrs. Robert C. Vose, III.

closing of the Ten Acre Yard may not have been seen as a permanent end to the launching of Weston vessels. But, in fact, it was.[1]

The end of shipbuilding, however, did not mean the end of the firm. Under the new name of E. Weston & Sons, the existing fleet continued to operate in their usual arenas, particularly the cotton trade. The master mariners who had become such a key part of the fleet's administration in King Caesar's day, including Captains Freeman Soule, Joseph Cummings, Lewis Peterson, Joshua Drew, and others, remained involved in the firm during the 1840s. While 1839 may have been the peak for Weston shipbuilding, the peak of its merchant trade was 1847, with more voyages completed and cargo moved than in any other year.

The chart on next page depicts the tonnage of the Weston fleet in the years between 1830 and 1857. As vessels were sold in the 1830s, they were replaced with larger vessels, the net result being an increase in the fleet's overall tonnage until 1842. The size of the fleet then remained roughly the same until 1849, when a marked decline began. The sons did not sell off vessels at a faster rate than before; indeed, the firm had always sold off two, even three ships every year.

Rather, they no longer replaced the vessels, evidently having made the decision not to maintain a fleet by the early 1850s.

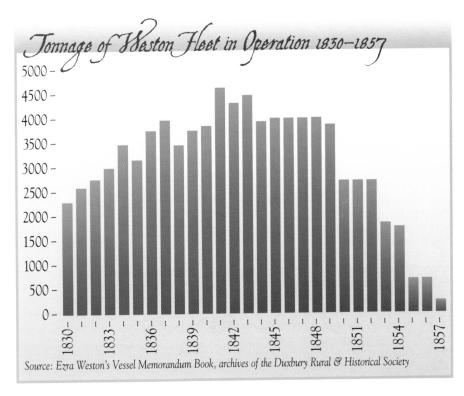

Tonnage of Weston Fleet in Operation 1830–1857

Source: Ezra Weston's Vessel Memorandum Book, archives of the Duxbury Rural & Historical Society

Most of the vessels were sold at the wharves of Boston, largely to merchants from the North Shore. Of the 12 buyers whose base of operations can be identified, 6 of them were from Salem.

As noted earlier, despite storms and pirate attacks, very few of the Weston's vessels were lost at sea. There are some notable exceptions. One was the schooner *Magnet* launched in 1838 which went aground on a sandbar at Aransas Bay, Texas in 1845. Another was the ship *Joshua Bates*, built by Samuel Hall in 1831, and named after an English merchant and philanthropist who was involved in Baring Brothers & Co. of London. After sailing for less than two years, the ship left Charleston and disappeared. Alden noted that she "sailed for Havre and was never heard from…She was spoken [hailed by another vessel] in the [English] channel. In fact a ship was seen to go on there by the same vessel that saw the *Joshua Bates* the day after they saw her in a gale of wind."[2]

Perhaps even more mystifying was the fate of the schooner *Volunteer*. While on a voyage to Puerto Rico in 1834, she suffered the loss of her foremast. Her master, rather than attempt repairs, simply abandoned the vessel at sea, perhaps deeming it dangerous to try to get her into port. After leaving the vessel, the crew somehow managed to get to nearby Bermuda. While the master moved on, the crew waited in Bermuda, keeping an eye out for the abandoned schooner, expecting her to drift on shore soon after their arrival. When she did a month later, the crew rushed to claim her, fully within their rights, and split the profit. In another rare show of personal opinion in his memorandum book, an agitated Alden B. Weston commented on the episode, "Was a bad operation and ought not to have been done…It was a poor affair of said captain's leaving her." Then, he added later in pencil as if the former remark were not clear enough, "He ought not to have done it."[3]

Gershom B. Weston

King Caesar's eldest son sat on the steps of Duxbury's First Parish Church engaged in an uncomfortable conversation with Captain Jacob Smith. Gershom was a big man and had inherited his mother's red hair. Captain Smith was about 20 years Gershom's elder. Now retired, Smith had sailed ships for Gershom's father; indeed, he was the same captain whose vessel had been boarded and burned by the French 30 years before. He was now exhibiting the same temper he had shown to the French captain.

Gershom Weston had encouraged abolition meetings in Duxbury, to which Smith objected "violently." Gershom, affirming his widely known opinion, stated that he should like to see more such meetings in the town.

Smith turned to him and pointed to the door of the church, asking if Gershom would "consent for the devil and hell to enter there."

No, Weston told him, he did not desire to see an abolition meeting held in the church. There were other places for that.[4]

Years later, however, Gershom would encourage meetings related to other reform movements to be held at the church. Smith was not the only one who reacted with indignation to Gershom's promotion of radical causes. There would be a backlash.

Gershom Bradford Weston (1799-1869), oldest son of King Caesar. This early photograph, probably taken in the late 1840s, shows Weston during the height of his involvement in the temperance and antislavery movements in Duxbury.

Photograph courtesy of
William Bradford Drury

Gershom Bradford Weston, c. 1865. "Uncle Gersh" (as he was known to many Duxbury soldiers in the Civil War) did what he could to ease the hardships of those men he had recruited to serve at the front.

According to family tradition, in the 1820s Gershom undertook management of the Weston's "outdoor" affairs, overseeing the shipyard and farms, about the time Alden took on the counting house. As a younger man, Gershom had been to sea on his father's ships as both as a captain's clerk and a second mate. While Alden's efforts, due to their clerical nature, are well documented, the extent of Gershom's direct involvement in the firm is unclear. It seems, perhaps, that he invested more time in the practice of politics.[5]

In this endeavor Gershom had a good deal of success. In 1828 he was elected to the Massachusetts House of Representatives, serving until 1831 and then again from 1834 to 1839. He served in the Massachusetts Senate from 1832 to 1833 and again from 1868 to 1869. And he was appointed to the Governor's council in 1852. Gershom also occupied a number of posts in Plymouth County government and served as Duxbury Town Moderator for 17 years. Still, he had higher political aspirations. In 1854 he ran for Congress on the Free-Soil ticket advocating the limitation of slavery. He lost the election by only 150 votes. Later, President Lincoln offered him the ambassadorship to Australia, which, for reasons unknown, he declined.[6]

In 1820, Gershom married Judith Sprague, the daughter of shipbuilder Seth Sprague. It was from his father-in-law that many of Gershom's radical views most likely originated. Sprague was a signer of the constitution of the Massachusetts Antislavery Society and later a Vice-President of the organization. He was a disciple of William Lloyd Garrison, Boston's eminent abolitionist, and stood by Garrison even as he came under attack by other abolitionists for his refusal to fight slavery in the arena of politics. In 1823 Sprague was irritated that the church in Duxbury would not espouse the moral views of antislavery, so he funded the construction of a new church on land fronting Washington Street, which he donated. When the new congregation also waffled on the matter, Sprague funded a third church, which was built in front of the second.

Gershom pursued the causes promoted by Seth Sprague. In the same spirit, he later threw his enthusiastic support behind the effort to preserve the Union in 1861. Too old to serve at the front, Gershom sent two sons to war and became an organizer of "war meetings" in Duxbury to recruit soldiers. His eloquence convinced many a Duxbury father and son to join the ranks. Once at the front, these men appealed to "Uncle Gersh" when needs arose. Gershom did what he could to improve their conditions by sending food, money, and clothing.[7]

Gershom and his wife set up house in 1820 on an attractive estate on Harmony Street, now St. George Street, next to a store owned by the Weston firm. In 1840, he built a sizeable mansion on the property, and lived there until 1850. In this new mansion Gershom lived the life one might expect of the son of King Caesar. He hosted large parties every summer for his Boston friends. Occasionally he took them out on the *Mayflower*, the 24-ton fishing yacht owned by the firm. He had barns filled with fine animals and a boathouse at the Old Cove with two spritsail boats. He was fond of hunting. In an 1851 publication it was said of Gershom, "He is generous, hospitable, fond of good living, more fond of having his own way, and

The Gershom B. Weston House, better known as the Wright Estate. Built about 1857 on the site of his previous house, which burned, the new house brought Weston financial trouble. The mansard roof and other enlargements were added by the Wright Family, which owned the house from 1868 to 1919.

pretty sure to have it…. If he had many more faults than he has, his general and unostentatious charity would cover them all."[8]

Indeed Gershom was charitable. Each Thanksgiving, for example, he distributed turkeys to an untold number of Duxbury families. He often gave money to those of the community in need, much to Alden's chagrin. Gershom's great generosity, combined with his predisposition for the good life, was a recipe for financial trouble.

A personal disaster made the mix more volatile in 1850 when his fine mansion burned. The fire began at midnight. After seeing that his numerous children were out of the building (he eventually had 13 and there were probably 9 in the house at that time) Gershom and his neighbors tried to salvage what little they could. They hurled furniture, carpets, and curtains from the front parlors out the windows. Two busts of George Washington and Daniel Webster dropped to the lawn. A maid who had been told to watch five-year-old Alden Weston, his uncle's namesake, went back in to retrieve some of her personal belongings. Once inside she was shocked to turn around and see that little Alden had followed her back

With dramatic drives leading to the house, the Wright Estate was known for its opulence. By the mid-20th century, the grandeur of the estate had faded. The property was donated to the Town by William P. Ellison and Harriet Rogers for a new high school and the house was removed.

into the burning house, obeying his orders to stay by her. Fortunately Alden was rescued with only his hair singed. No one had been hurt, but almost everything was lost, including cash and family papers. Even Gershom's all important spectacles.[9]

Mirroring his public life, the fire took place at the height of Gershom's involvement in a community controversy. For years, Gershom had encouraged meetings of abolitionists and temperance activists. One of his followers was Mary Ashton Rice Livermore, the wife of the Universalist minister in Duxbury. A bold organizer and abolitionist, she went on to coordinate the efforts of the U.S. Sanitary Commission in Chicago during the Civil War. Of her days in Duxbury and the temperance movement, Livermore later wrote:

> The town of Duxbury, like almost every town and city of New England, was brought under the spell of this mighty moral influence. A Total Abstinence Society was formed, that included most of the adult population, while a "Cold Water Army" was recruited from the children. Hon. Gershom Weston, the wealthiest and most influential man of the town at that time, was the president of the adult organization, and I was pressed into work for the children. It was the first temperance work of my life, in which I have continued to the present day. To maintain an interest among the little people, frequent meetings were necessary, which must be made attractive, with music and recitation and brief stirring speeches.[10]

While such meetings were inspirational to some, they were deeply disturbing to others. In the views of a more conservative element, Weston crossed a line when he invited antislavery activist Theodore Parker to speak in Duxbury. Summing up the views of his opposition, Weston later stated that he was despised because he had introduced "into this town…a man whose principles border on infidelity." His irate critics, Weston said, felt that it would take many years to eradicate

Parker's "pernicious influences." Weston faced so much animosity from the members of his church that he left the congregation around 1846 and joined the church that his father-in-law had established.[11]

In 1850, when Weston sought to give a temperance lecture in the very church that he had criticized and quit, it was more than many could stand. The resulting war of words was bitter and long. Seeking to defend his character, Weston organized a public meeting at the old Town Hall, which was attended by a huge number of people. During the meeting, he enumerated in detail the accusations leveled at him, and refuted them one by one. Weston's posturing during the meeting, transcribed in full by a Boston "phonographer" sent to the meeting by Weston's opponents, clearly reveals his desire to maintain his influence over local politics.

One of the accusations was that Weston had led the church into building an expensive new meeting house which resulted in debt. Another was that, in Weston's words, "[Weston] lives luxuriously, but thinks the poor minister can live upon a reduced salary." And another accusation, again summarized in Weston's words, was that, "It is well known that [Weston] is of an uneasy disposition, constantly advancing some new scheme for the public, and thereby involving himself and those around him in difficulty."[12]

During his refutation, Weston continually referred to the fact that his opponents had accused him of making "tools" of others. His opponents argued that they had never actually used this term. Regardless, the key issues revolved around Weston's attempts to exert his influence in various matters whether social, political, or economic. The Kings Caesar, his father and grandfather, acting in times of prosperity, could get away with this. In an era of economic decline, Gershom B. Weston could not. Duxbury would have no more kings.

Following the fire that consumed his home, and the political flames that so damaged his local credibility, Gershom Weston moved his family to a home on the corner of Boylston and Church Streets in Boston's new Back Bay. Seven years later, in 1857, he felt it was time to return to Duxbury. To the surprise of many, Gershom built a new mansion atop the ashes of his old. This house, not quite as elaborate as its predecessor, stood on St. George Street well into the 20th century. Purchased in 1868 and enlarged by the Wright Family, it was better known as the Wright Estate.

Sadly, the construction of an expensive new mansion did not prove to be a wise choice. Gershom found himself in debt, in large part to his brother Alden who still occupied King Caesar's house on Powder Point. A terrible rift was in the making.

Ezra Weston IV

Although King Caesar's youngest son Ezra Weston IV was made a full partner with his brothers a few months before their father's death, he had never had a great deal to do with the administration of the fleet. He was fond of travel and very much involved in Boston society. These interests prevented him from playing an active role in the Weston firm, and he apparently preferred to entrust matters to his older brothers.

As a boy, Ezra's health was poor. He suffered from rheumatic fever and never fully recovered from the effects of rheumatism, at times in his life suffering great pain. In 1836, when Ezra was 25, King Caesar noted that, "Doctor Bowditch recommends for Ezra to go to sea, a London voyage."[13] Whether this was for reasons of health, or experience, or both is unclear. Ezra enjoyed travel, especially to Paris, which he visited a number of times in the 1840s and 1850s. He had his photograph taken in a Paris studio about 1849, one of the earliest Weston family photographs.

Ezra IV was the first Weston to receive a college education, joining Harvard's class of 1829. He was popular among his fellow students, who elected him to command the college's military company. This was the beginning of Ezra's lifelong connection to Boston social circles. After his graduation, he made something of a profession of serving in honorific positions. He was City Marshall of Boston, deputy sheriff of Suffolk County, and Captain of the Boston Light Infantry, known as the "Boston Tigers."

He had diverse interests and the leisure to explore them. He became involved in a number of social causes in Boston including the Boston Society for the Prevention of Pauperism, of which he was secretary. He was also a talented musician.

Ezra Weston IV (1809-1852). The photograph was taken in a Paris studio in the late 1840s.

The portrait below was painted c. 1829.

Ezra dabbled in horticulture, visiting Parisian gardens and bringing back specimens. In 1836, he was honored with the invitation to address the annual meeting of the Massachusetts Horticultural Society. In his remarks, Weston shows something of a transcendentalist leaning (he corresponded with Ralph Waldo Emerson), evidently influenced by the cultural movement taking hold in Massachusetts at the time. "There are few things more refreshing to the man of business, or to any man," Weston said, "that will so recruit the senses and charm the spirit as to step aside a moment from the confusion and anxiety of the street and look upon the beauty and bounty of nature...He who cultivates a garden and brings perfection to flowers and fruits, cultivates and advances at the same time his own nature."[14]

Weston planted many trees on Powder Point, unwittingly providing shade and beautiful scenery for many students at the Powder Point School for Boys that would one day occupy his father's estate.

Ezra IV died of apoplexy, or stroke, in the King Caesar House in 1852. He was 42 years old.

Alden B. Weston

My Ships

This compass rose, drawn by Alden B. Weston in 1853, appears as the graphic element at the beginning of each chapter in this book.

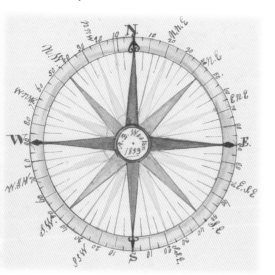

"How many ships with silken sails
   I've launched upon the sea,
When glittering waters kissed their keels
   And seraph gales were free!
I've seen them start for cloudless climes
   Along a star-bright way;
Alas! these waiting eyes of mine—
   Where are my ships today?

I scan the sea-encircled shore:
   No ship rocks at its piers;
No pennons fly along the sky;
   The wintry chill of years

Moans at my heart, at night, at morn;

Still through the bickering rain

I'm watching for my silken sails

That never come again." [15]

Alden B. Weston closed the doors of the Weston counting house on Commercial Wharf on December 31, 1857. Aged 52, he set about making the transition to a

Alden Bradford Weston (1805-1880) photographed around 1870. While there are numerous surviving photographs of his older brother Gershom, this is the only known image of Alden.

life of leisure. For a time he continued to live at a boarding house in Boston, enjoying, it is said, frequent evening games of whist with his fellow boarders. At some point around 1858, Alden began living in his father's house on Powder Point year round, about the same time that his brother Gershom moved back to Duxbury. In 1860, Alden married Phebe Aderton of Freeport, Maine. They were wed in St. Louis. Phebe died in Duxbury in 1869, leaving Alden to live in the King Caesar House alone for the next 11 years.

It seems that Alden had few interests beyond business. To some extent, he shared his younger brother's curiosity for the study of natural science. A typical letter of instruction from his father to one of his ship's captains has an unusual footnote penned in by a 28 year-old Alden, "Capt Sprague, Sir, I wish you would just bear in mind to bring me any curiosity that you may come in contact with, whether of the earth, air or the sea, provided they do not come at too dear a cost. Yours, AB Weston." This was the primary difference between Alden and his brothers: pursuit of curiosity, but not at too dear a cost. He lived simply. When, in the mid-1850s, Gershom suggested that the two surviving brothers begin the construction of clipper ships in Boston, Alden refused. The brothers did not quite see eye to eye, but still they were, according to Gershom's youngest son, on "brotherly and friendly terms" before 1861. [16]

Prior to the rift, Uncle Alden had a pleasant relationship with his nieces and nephews, Gershom's children. One of them recalled, "Many a Christmas morning,

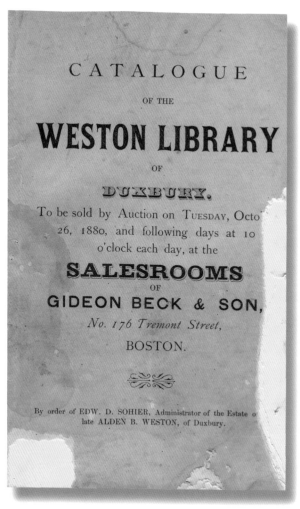

on account of his generosity and thoughtfulness, he greatly added to my pleasure and to that of my youngest half-brother and my two half-sisters by our finding many attractive presents in our stockings that were hung up the night before." [17]

The sad schism between Gershom and Alden began in 1861. Gershom's new house on Harmony Street strained his weak financial situation, which had not fully recovered from the loss of his former house years before. Alden lent him money. As Gershom spiraled further into debt, Alden soon held the mortgage on the Harmony Street estate. With Gershom continuing to enjoy the same extravagant lifestyle, at some point Alden decided that enough was enough. He foreclosed on his brother.

Gershom's youngest son later wrote, "It is with sorrow that I recall the unpleasant events which transpired during the last six or eight years of my father's life, as the two brothers were deeply estranged…The final result was that after about six years of litigation…my father, in due process of law, was evicted from his home by his brother under trying circumstances in the winter of 1867 and was obliged to move into a small house which he rented nearby." [18]

Before the eviction, while Gershom and his family still resided in their mansion, Alden placed the estate on the market in 1865. "For sale," read the advertisement in the *Old Colony Memorial*, "an elegant residence…about 30 acres of land… the house is large, is heated by a furnace, has water closet and other modern conveniences. The grounds are beautifully laid out, with orchards and ornamental trees…and the tillage is good and conveniently located. A very desirable country residence for any person wishing one. Will be sold cheap." To Gershom, the final line must have been a harsh twist. [19]

One can only surmise how Alden came to such a severe decision. It must have been frustrating to see the firm's fortune spent so swiftly by his brothers. No matter how generous Gershom's charitable activities, Alden probably considered legal action necessary to preserve what he, his father, and his grandfather had worked so hard to establish. In the resulting settlement, most of Gershom's assets were turned over to Alden. The smaller house to which Gershom and his second wife Deborah Brownell Weston moved, adjacent to and within sight of his old mansion, still stands on Pine Hill Lane. The house was purchased for Gershom and family by his colleagues in the Massachusetts Senate. For the next two years, until his death in 1869, Gershom saw the gradual transformations in his estate as George and Georgianna Wright, soon to become Duxbury's most influential family of the late 19th century, enlarged the house and improved the grounds.

There was no reconciliation between the brothers. After Gershom's death in 1869, the same year as Alden's wife's, Alden was virtually shunned by his nieces and nephews. During the 1870s, he kept primarily to the King Caesar House. There were at least two other residents of the house at that time, Hannah Sullivan and Kate O'Brien, both Irish domestic servants. Hannah served at the King Caesar House for more than 11 years.[20]

Due to his reclusive habits and his apparently callous treatment of his brother, Alden gained a somewhat grim reputation in Duxbury. One tale, whether true or not, demonstrates local perceptions. After the Civil War, a new generation of determined young men attempted shipbuilding in Duxbury. Nathaniel Porter Keene and William Paulding were the two most successful, but even they were only moderately so. Keene had taken over the yard formerly belonging to Levi Sampson on the Bluefish River, with King Caesar's old Ten Acre Yard

*The shipyard of Nathaniel Porter Keene in Duxbury with the ship **Samuel G. Reed** on the stocks, looking north towards Powder Point Avenue along the Bluefish River (1869). Builders Keene and Paulding successfully launched several large vessels in Duxbury after the Civil War, but they were unable to rekindle the glory days of Duxbury shipbuilding.*

Porter Keene's Ship Yard
Duxbury, Mass
Ship Samuel G. Reed on stocks. Built in 1869

on his east and the Harmony Bridge hard by on his west. The older carpenters who had worked the yards during the antebellum period knew all too well the challenges of the shallow harbor and chided the new builders on their attempts to create a shipbuilding renaissance. Keene's largest vessel, the *Henry J. Lippett*, was referred to as "Keene's Elephant." When the attempt was made to launch her in 1874, she stuck on the ways and the old timers joked that she was trying to get back on land where she belonged.

When the ship was finally dislodged, she slammed 40 feet into the opposite bank of the river. With some difficulty, she was floated again and then secured to a tree on Alden Weston's property. Irritated by the damage done to his tree, Alden allegedly came out of the King Caesar House and cast off the line when it was unsupervised, allowing the *Henry J. Lippett* to drift and run aground on the opposite bank.

Furious, Keene paid a visit to Weston and a heated discussion ensued. When Alden pointed out the damage to his tree, Keene retorted that his vessel was in distress and had a right to use any means to ensure her safety. Weston dryly responded that since Mr. Keene's vessel had not yet been to sea, she could not be a vessel in distress. Keene had no response to this narrow-mindedness. A year later he moved his shipyard to Weymouth.[21]

In this and other satirical bits of folklore, Alden became a negative caricature. Though not as loud as the criticism leveled at his brother Gershom in the 1850s, the negative rumors generated about Alden by his neighbors in the 1870s are indicative of the same disillusionment Duxbury folk felt towards the Weston family during the depressed decades following Duxbury's golden era of shipbuilding. Unlike Gershom who vociferously defended his character, Alden quietly withdrew.

One by one, Alden had the industrial buildings on the King Caesar property taken down or removed. The last remnant of the ropewalk, the headhouse fronting today's King Caesar Road, was taken down in 1862. His great-grandfather Eliphas's house was torn down in 1863. The wharf buildings were removed and the fields out back, farmed as late as the 1860s, were eventually left to grass and weeds.

Alden died on June 1, 1880. His nieces and nephews inherited the estate. But the daunting task of restoring it, and the aforementioned rumors that a will somewhere existed in which Alden left the property to the First Parish Church, kept them from taking an active interest in the house. There are indications that they used the property from time to time, but for the most part it sat neglected.

Until it was discovered six years later by Frederick B. Knapp on an August day.

EPILOGUE

The Legacy

On June 25, 1967, members of the Duxbury Rural and Historical Society and the community at large gathered at King Caesar's house to celebrate its dedication as a museum. Seating was set up on the manicured lawn where once had been the shabby, miniature forest of poplar saplings through which Frederick Knapp had strode. To the west of the house on the ropewalk lot now stood 20th century houses. Several of the barns behind the house were now summer residences. King Caesar's wharf had already been gifted to the Society in 1946 by Hermon C. Bumpus, Jr. to serve as a park dedicated to the memory of his father who had restored the house in the 1930s. Now known as Bumpus Park, the wharf still affords the same majestic view of Duxbury Bay once enjoyed by King Caesar.

The Bumpus family sold the King Caesar House in 1945 to Elizabeth Weber-Fulop, a Viennese artist who had left Austria during World War II. After twenty years of ownership, she offered the house for sale in the winter of 1965. At a meeting of the Duxbury Rural and Historical Society on April 26, 1965, Society President William Nash announced, according to the local paper,

> …that a rare opportunity had presented itself to acquire for the Society…this beautiful and historic house…It would become a landmark commemorative of the busy ship building days of Duxbury… Accordingly, a group of Duxbury people met to discuss this matter. They were asked for their reaction as to whether or not steps be taken to secure this property so that…it could be preserved permanently as an outstanding Duxbury landmark, to be owned, maintained and occupied as the Society's headquarters, for the citizens of Duxbury. The response was most enthusiastic and unanimously favorable.[1]

Weston family coat of arms from the gravestone of Ezra Weston II. The motto, Craignez Honte, means, "Fear Shame."

Society member Garwen Bawden chaired a fundraising committee and a campaign was launched in September 1965. By Thanksgiving the goal of $128,000 needed for the purchase and restoration of the house had been raised. After two years of restorative work, both inside and out, the house exhibited the same grandeur as it had during the days of Ezra Weston II, 125 years earlier.

Since 1967 the King Caesar House has been maintained by the Duxbury Rural and Historical Society as a museum "commemorative of the busy ship building days of Duxbury," and to the accomplishments of King Caesar in particular. Represented as it may have appeared about 1820, the house is filled with local furnishings and artifacts from King Caesar's era. It is indeed a landmark, and a point of pride for the community.

The legacy preserved within the King Caesar House is one of tremendous achievement. By establishing a context of growth and change in the patterns of shipbuilding on the South Shore, we see the Weston enterprise was truly unique in its region of the Commonwealth. Although they probably were not Webster's "largest shipowners in the United States," they operated on a scale unmatched in Plymouth County, dramatic in their supremacy, one of the most significant enterprises in Massachusetts maritime history.

It is also a story of personal character. The firm's distinction was achieved primarily by the younger King Caesar, Ezra Weston II, who, by gathering about him the region's best builders and master mariners, built upon his father's foundation and created a premier fleet known throughout the Atlantic. The subtleties of King Caesar's talent and ability have become buried underneath the autocratic persona of legend. Weston's skill for managing both people and money, his bold choices in capitalizing on uncertain and sometimes controversial markets, and his driving ambition were the key factors in the firm's achievements. His role is further emphasized by the fact that the power and prestige of the family crumbled so rapidly after his death.

It is a legacy worth preserving.

Appendix

Ezra Weston's Early Fleet, 1764–1799

Vessel Name	Vessel Type	Year Built	Place Built	Year Sold	Tonnage	Known Co-owners	Master Carpenter	Known Masters
Dolphin	Sloop	1764						
Silvia	Sloop	1767				Warren Weston		
Fair Lady	Schooner	1770						
Ranger	Schooner	1771			82			J. Simmons
Sally	Schooner	1771						
Albanus	Schooner	1781						
Congress	Sloop	1783			80	George Partridge		Ezra Weston I William Kent
Humbird	Schooner	1784				Daniel Sargent		
Eagle	Schooner	1785	Duxbury		62			Joshua Brewster Peleg Kent
Sophia	Schooner	1786	Duxbury		25	Barzillai Delano Darius Brewster		Barzillai Delano Darius Brewster
Phoenix	Schooner	1788	Duxbury		53			Thomas Chandler Daniel Hall
Prissy	Schooner	1789			53	Seth Byram		Daniel Hall Asa Weston
Lark	Sloop	1789						
Friendship	Sloop	1789						
Columbia	Sloop	1794			52			J. Clarke Daniel Hall
Rising Sun	Brigantine	1796			141			S. Blackmer Daniel Bradford
Rising States	Schooner	1797			73			Daniel Bradford

Vessel Name	Vessel Type	Year Built	Place Built	Year Sold	Tonnage	Known Co-owners	Master Carpenter	Known Masters
Pomona	Sloop	1797						
Volant	Schooner	1798			73			Seth Simmons
Jerusha	Sloop	1798						
Sylvia	Brig	1798			130			
Berin	Schooner	1799						
Laurel	Schooner	1799						
Union	Schooner	1799						

The Middle Fleet, 1800–1824

Vessel Name	Vessel Type	Year Built	Place Built	Year Sold	Tonnage	Known Co-owners	Master Carpenter	Known Masters
Federal Eagle	Brig	1800	Duxbury		141	Warren Weston	T. Southworth	Luke Hall
Levant	Brig	1800			144			
Maria	Sloop	1801	Haverhill		88			Edward D. Baker
Admittance	Brigantine	1802	Duxbury		170	Isaac Hatch	Calvin Sampson	Calvin Sampson Joseph Collins
Fame	Sloop	1803						
Julius Caesar	Ship	1804	Haverhill		300	Luke Hall	John Kendrick	Luke Hall Paul Post
Ezra & Daniel	Brig	1805	Duxbury		169	Daniel Hall	Joshua Magoun	Daniel Hall
Fenelon	Schooner	1806	Duxbury		108			Benjamin Linnell
Gershom	Brig	1806	Duxbury		112		Joshua Magoun	Joshua Hall Luther Pierce 1809 Jacob Smith 1811-12
Salumith	Schooner	1806	Duxbury		111			John Brown
Apollo	Sloop	1807						
Minerva	Ship	1808	Duxbury		223	Calvin Sampson		William Snow Ephraim Safford
Admittance	Ship	1809	Kingston		238	Jacob Weston Phineas Sprague		Phineas Sprague John McGlathlin
Linnet	Sloop	1809			50			
Warren	Brig	1809	Duxbury		184	Jacob Weston	John Oldham	Warren Weston
Flora	Schooner	1810	Duxbury			Jacob Weston	Jacob Weston	Gershom Bradford
Ardent	Schooner	1811			125			
Camillus	Ship	1811	Duxbury		337	John Howland	James Southworth	John Howland
George Washington	Schooner	1812						
Cossack	Schooner	1813						

Vessel Name	Vessel Type	Year Built	Place Built	Year Sold	Tonnage	Known Co-owners	Master Carpenter	Known Masters
Dispatch	Brig	1815	Duxbury		136			Jacob Smith
Golden Grove	Brig	1815	Duxbury		134			Daniel Hall
Linnet	Sloop	1815			69			
Triton	Schooner	1815			52			
Bramin	Ship	1816	Duxbury		245			W. MacGregor
Exchange	Sloop	1816	Duxbury		56	Asa Sampson		Thomas Chandler
Messenger	Brig	1816	Duxbury		135			James Harding Job E. Brewster 1825 Zara Higgins 1836 Nathaniel Loring 1836-1838 Alexander Mayo 1839-1840 Benjamin Smith 1843-1844 Elijah Sampson 1844-1849
Diamond	Sloop	1817			44			
St. Michael	Schooner	1817			120			Nathaniel Soule John Bartram
Angler	Schooner	1818			48			
Collector	Schooner	1818	Duxbury		91	George Loring Benjamin Bates		Nathaniel Soule
Dispatch	Brig	1818	Duxbury		124			Nathaniel Simmons Jr.
Franklin	Schooner	1819			60			
Two Friends	Brig	1819	Duxbury		260	Abraham Barker	George Loring	Jacob Smith
Margaret	Brig	1820	Scituate		185	Elisha Foster, Jr. of Scituate	Samuel & Seth Foster	Martin Waterman 1820 E. Scudder 1830-31 Macdonald 1831-34 E. Wadsworth 1834 K.N. Gage 1835-38 Elijah Sampson 1838-39
Panope	Schooner	1820			92			Asa Rogers Benjamin Linnell 1822
Star	Schooner	1820			20			
Baltic	Brig	1821	Duxbury		212			Ezra Weston II Jacob Burgess
Globe	Brig	1822	Duxbury		214	Elijah Loring of Boston Jacob Smith	Levi Sampson	Jacob Smith 1822-34 E. Wadsworth 1834-36

Vessel Name	Vessel Type	Year Built	Place Built	Year Sold	Tonnage	Known Co-owners	Master Carpenter	Known Masters
Herald	Brig	1822	Duxbury		162		Benjamin Prior	Nathaniel Simmons 1822 Martin Waterman 1829 Zara Higgins 1832 Joseph Cummings 1832-34
Franklin	Ship	1825		Bef. 1830	246			
Pioneer	Brig	1825	Scituate	Bef. 1830	231	Benjamin Smith Seth Foster Samuel Foster	Seth Foster	Benjamin Smith 1825-1828
Pallas	Bark	1825	Duxbury	1832	209		Levi Sampson	George Winsor
Smyrna	Brig	1825	Marshfield	1838	162		Seth Foster	Seth F. Sprague 1825-29
Dray	Schooner	1825	Duxbury	Bef. 1830	86		Samuel A. Frazar	Simeon Soule 1825
Levant	Brig	c.1825		1834	219			Ichabod Simmons c.1830-1833 Lewis Peterson 1834
Lagoda	Ship	1826	Scituate	1833	340	Thomas Otis Seth Foster	Seth & Samuel Foster	Daniel Brewster
Ganges	Brig	1826	Duxbury	Bef. 1830	174	Daniel Pingree	Hall, Samuel	Simeon Soule 1826-28
Malaga	Brig	1827	Scituate	1832	150		Souther Cudworth	Isaac Simmons 1827 Zara Higgins c.1831-32
Pomona	Schooner	1827	Duxbury	Bef. 1830	84			Seth Wadsworth
Julian	Ship	1828	Duxbury	1835	356	Benjamin Smith	Samuel Hall	Benjamin Smith 1828-c.1830 Martin Waterman c.1830-1834
Ceres	Brig	1828	Duxbury	1836	176		Samuel Hall	Simeon Soule 1828 Zara Higgins 1832-33 Joseph Cummings 1834-1836
Virginia	Schooner	1828		Bef. 1830	73			J. David
Neptune	Brig	1829	Duxbury	1841	196	Robert Brookhouse	Samuel Hall	Simeon Soule 1829-34 N.K. Loring 1835-36 Joseph Cummings 1836-39 Josiah Knowles 1839-40 Alexander Mayo 1840-41
Slide	Sloop	1829		Bef. 1830	60			
Renown	Ship	1830	Duxbury	1832	295		Samuel Hall	Martin Waterman 1830

Vessel Name	Vessel Type	Year Built	Place Built	Year Sold	Tonnage	Known Co-owners	Master Carpenter	Known Masters
Seaman	Schooner	1830			70			
Joshua Bates	Ship	1831	Duxbury	1833	316		Samuel Hall	Job Brewster
Undine	Ship	1831		1844	253			Nathaniel Weston 1831-34 Freeman Soule 1834-36 B. Taylor 1836-39 David Cushman Jr. 1842
Minerva	Ship	1832	Duxbury	1844	291		Drew, Sylvanus	Seth F. Sprague 1832-35 William Weston 1835-37 Zaddock Bradford 1837-38 Alexander Wadsworth 1838-40 Joseph Cummings 1844
Angola	Brig	1832	Duxbury	1832	220	Edward Kimball	Samuel Hall	Ichabod Simmons
Sea Drift	Schooner	1832		1856	90		Samuel Hall	Samuel Walker
Mattakeesett	Ship	1833	Duxbury	1850	481		Samuel Hall	Briggs Thomas 1833 Seth F. Sprague 1838-39 Zara Higgins 1839-41 B. Taylor 1841-43 Gershom B. Weston Jr. 1844 David Cushman Jr. 1845 Joseph Cummings 1846-48 Lewis Peterson 1849-50
St. Lawrence	Ship	1833	Duxbury	1835	356		Samuel Hall	Otis Baker
Volunteer	Schooner	1833		1834	109			A. Hopkins
Admittance	Ship	1834	Duxbury	1842	426		Samuel Hall	Simeon Soule 1834 Zaddock Bradford 1834-37 Freeman Soule 1837 Benjamin Smith 1837-41
Messenger	Brig	1834	Duxbury	1849	213		Samuel Hall	Zara Higgins 1834-36 N.K. Loring 1836-38 Alexander Mayo 1839 B. Taylor 1840-41 Elisha Sampson 1843-44 Benjamin Smith 1844
Liberty	Schooner	1834			92			
Vandalia	Ship	1835	Duxbury	1843	434		Samuel Hall	Seth F. Sprague 1835-38 Alexander Wadsworth 1840-41 Church Weston 1841-43

Vessel Name	Vessel Type	Year Built	Place Built	Year Sold	Tonnage	Known Co-owners	Master Carpenter	Known Masters
Packet	Schooner	1835			70			
Eliza Warwick	Ship	1836	Duxbury	1839	530	Abraham Warwick	Samuel Hall	Robert Welch 1836-39
Trenton	Brig	1836	Duxbury	1855	226		Samuel Hall	Lewis Peterson 1836-37
Oriole	Brig	1837	Duxbury	1838	218		Samuel Cushing	Lewis Peterson 1837-38
Magnet	Schooner	1838		1846	80			Thomas F. Burgess
Oneco	Ship	1839	Duxbury	1855	640	Joshua Drew	Samuel Cushing	Joshua Drew 1839-43 B. Taylor 1843-44 Joshua Drew 1844-52 Gershom B. Weston Jr. 1854-55
Lion	Brig	1839	Duxbury	1857	235		Daniel Brewster	Alexander Mayo 1841-42 Lewis Peterson 1842-43 Elisha Sampson 1844 C. Watson 1844-45 Lewis Peterson 1845-46 Thomas Cunningham 1849-52 A.A. Gardner 1852-55 W. Merritt 1855 A.H. Sears 1856
Smyrna	Brig	1839	Duxbury	1855	196		Samuel Cushing	Joseph Cummings 1839-43 T. Gorham 1843-44 Lewis Peterson 1844-45
Reform	Sloop	1839			53			Isaac Simmons
Angler	Schooner	1840		1854	86			
Hope	Ship	1841	Duxbury	1853	880		Samuel Cushing	Freeman Soule 1841-48 Gershom Weston Jr. 1848-50 John Bradford 1850-53
Vulture	Brig	1842	Duxbury	1856	140			Alexander Mayo 1845-46 Andrew Burditt 1849-52 Hiram Perkins 1853-55
Manteo	Ship	1843	Duxbury	1850	599		Samuel Cushing	Joshua Drew 1843-44 Otis Baker 1844-47 T. Laighton 1847-50
Mayflower	Schooner	1844						
Ocean	Schooner	1845		1856	103			
Express	Schooner	1846		1856	93			Robert Stoddard

Sources: Ship Registers of the District of Plymouth, Massachusetts, 1789-1908 (National Archives Project, 1939); E. Weston's Vessel Memorandum Book, "Weston Collection," Duxbury Rural and Historical Society, Box 4; list of vessels compiled by Alden B. Weston, II, "Weston Collection," Box 13.

Prologue

1 Frederick Bradford Knapp, Diary 1886, Frederick B. Knapp Papers, archives of the Duxbury Rural and Historical Society. See also Lucia Knapp Royal, "King Caesar House," "Weston Collection," archives of the Duxbury Rural and Historical Society, Box 8, p. 7.

2 Dorothy Wentworth, *Settlement and Growth of Duxbury* (Duxbury: Duxbury Rural and Historical Society, 2000), p. 133.

3 Quoted in Edmund B. Weston *In Memoriam: Hon. Gershom Bradford Weston and Deborah Brownell Weston* (Published by Edmund B. Weston, 1916), p. 13.

4 Henry Howe, Massachusetts, *There She Is—Behold Her!* (Harper & Brothers, 1960), p. 160-1.

5 Bernard and Lotte Bailyn, *Massachusetts Shipping 1697-1714: A Statistical Study* (Cambridge: Belknap Press of the Harvard University Press, 1959), p. v.

Chapter One: *Ancestors*

1 James Camden Hotten, *The Original Lists of Persons of Quality* (New York: Empire State Book Co., 1874), pp. 57-58, 69, 72, 76-78.

2 Thomas Weston, Jr., *The Descendants of Edmund Weston of Duxbury* (Boston: George E. Littlefield, 1887), p. 5. See also Eugene A. Stratton, "The Descendants of Edmund Weston of Duxbury Revisited," National Genealogical Society Quarterly, Vol. 71 (Mar. 1983), p. 42.

3 Francis J. Bremer, *The Puritan Experiment: New England Society from Bradfords to Edwards* (Hanover: University Press of New England, 1995), pp. 38-45.

4 Ibid. p. 42. For more on comparative migration to Massachusetts and Virginia see Roger Thompson, *Mobility and Migration: East Anglian Founders of New England* (University of Massachusetts Press, 1994), p. 122.

5 Hotten, *The Original Lists*, pp. 57-58, 69, 72, 76-78.

6 Stratton, "Descendants of Edmund Weston," p. 42.

7 For more on indentured servitude in Plymouth Colony see Eugene A. Stratton, *Plymouth Colony: Its History and People 1620-1691* (Salt Lake City: Ancestry Publishing, 1986), pp. 179-189.

8 Justin Winsor, *History of Duxbury* (Boston: Crosby & Nichols, 1849), p. 171.

9 Stratton, "Descendants of Edmund Weston," p. 42.

10 Samuel N. Weston, "Genealogies of the Weston Family of Duxbury," unpublished typescript at the Duxbury Free Library, p. 30. George Etheridge ed., *Records of the Town of Duxbury 1642-1770* (Plymouth, MA: Avery & Doten, 1893), p. 58.

11 Bernard and Lotte Bailyn, *Massachusetts Shipping 1697-1714: A Statistical Study* (Cambridge: Belknap Press of the Harvard University Press, 1959), p. 85.

12 Ezra Weston III [sic], "Weston Family of Duxbury, Mass," manuscript collection of the New England Historic and Genealogical Society, p. 145. According to a notation on the cover of this manuscript, which contains many interesting anecdotes about the Weston family, the work is attributed to Ezra Weston, III. However, the work contains information post-dating the death of Ezra Weston (1809-1852), youngest son of "King Caesar." It is possible that the work was assembled by Thomas Weston, Jr. who was at the time preparing to publish a genealogy on the Weston family.

13 Dorothy Wentworth, "John Weston House," dateboard files of the Duxbury Rural and Historical Society, n.d.

14 Dorothy Wentworth, "Weston Family before 1808," manuscript, archives of the Duxbury Rural and Historical Society, n.d.

15 Henry Howe, Massachusetts, *There She Is—Behold Her!* (Harper & Brothers, 1960), p. 68-70.

16 Ezra Weston III [sic], "Weston Family of Duxbury, Mass," p. 124 and 146. According to a notation, the information of the deaths of Eliphas and sons was supplied by Alden Bradford Weston, second son of Ezra Weston, Jr.

17 Nathaniel Weston, "Notes on Powder Point," manuscript, archives of the Duxbury Rural and Historical Society, 1909, p. 5.

Chapter Two: *Father*

1 The details of this tale, probably folklore, are taken from Edward Harvey Sampson, "Some Items Relative to the History and Development of Duxbury," archives of the Duxbury Rural and Historical Society, 1906), p. 19. In that paper, Sampson records the recollections of

several ship captains still living who knew Ezra Weston II, so the popular story may have a kernel of truth. It may be of interest to note that a 19th-century source, an undated note by Mary Nye Gifford in the "King Caesar" file in the Duxbury Rural and Historical Society archives, also notes that King Caesar often wore a red cloak.

2 Ezra Weston to Arunah Weston, in a letter dated July 22, 1771, "Weston Collection," archives of the Duxbury Rural and Historical Society, Box 6, folder 1.

3 Unknown author to Ezra Weston, April 21, 1774, Ezra Weston I Papers, archives of the Duxbury Rural and Historical Society, folder "EW 1770s."

4 Account statement, "Ezra Weston debtor to Mungo Mackay," March 25, 1774, Ezra Weston I Papers, folder "EW 1770s."

5 Ezra Weston to Warren Weston, n.d., "Weston Collection," Box 6, folder 1.

6 Indenture, Amos Sampson to Ezra Weston, 1773, Ezra Weston I Papers, folder "Legal Matters."

7 Justin Winsor, *History of Duxbury*, p. 120.

8 Ibid., p. 122.

9 Ibid., p. 127.

10 Ibid., pp. 129-130. See also Cynthia Krussel, *Of Tea and Tories* (Marshfield Bicentennial Committee, 1976).

11 *Massachusetts Soldiers and Sailors in the War of the Revolution* (Boston: Wright and Potter Printing Co., State Printers), vol. X, page 110. Justin Winsor, History of Duxbury, p. 144.

12 Samuel Eliot Morison, *Maritime History of Massachusetts* (Boston: Houghton Mifflin Company, 1961), p. 31.

13 Robert G. Albion, William A. Baker, and Benjamin W. Labaree, eds, *New England and the Sea* (Mystic, CT: Mystic Seaport Museum, Inc., 1994), pp. 54-56.

14 Robert Pope to Ezra Weston, in a letter dated April 16, 1781, Ezra Weston I Papers, folder "EW 1780-83."

15 Emma Worcester Sargent and Charles Sprague Sargent, *Epes Sargent of Gloucester and his Descendants* (Boston and New York: Houghton Mifflin Company, 1923), pp. 137-138.

16 Statements from Daniel Sargent, Ezra Weston I Papers, folders EW 1784, 1785, 1786, 1790.

17 Statements from Daniel Sargent, Ezra Weston I Papers, folder "EW 1789."

18 Detailed Fish Fairs, indicating the value of catches, were kept by skippers. This data was taken from Ezra Weston I Papers, folders "Schooner Prissy," "Schooner Sophia," "Schooner Eagle."

19 Katherine Pillsbury, "The Westons: Duxbury's Caesars," in *The Duxbury Book* (Duxbury Rural and Historical Society, 1987) p. 62.

20 Account of the schooner Phoenix, Ezra Weston I Papers, folder "Schooner Phoenix."

21 Statements of account, Ezra Weston I Papers, folder "EW 1795-6"; accounts of Captain Henry Chandler, folder "Schooner Prissy."

22 Samuel Eliot Morison, *Maritime History of Massachusetts* (Boston: Houghton Mifflin, 1961), p. 144.

23 Data on the early fleet is assembled primarily from records in the Ezra Weston I Papers. See also the list of vessels compiled by Alden B. Weston, II, "Weston Collection," archives of the Duxbury Rural and Historical Society, Box 13; *Ship Registers of the District of Plymouth, Massachusetts 1789-1908* (National Archives Project, 1939). Tonnage is not recorded for all early vessels and so in some cases an average of 61 tons per vessel has been assumed based on available data.

24 Justin Winsor, *History of Duxbury*, p. 350. Data on other builders is from Registers of the District of Plymouth, Massachusetts.

25 This data is here shown to give some indication of the number of vessels *operating* out of Plymouth County ports at the time. This is not a complete picture of vessels *built* on the South Shore. There were, in fact, many more vessels built in Plymouth County than are indicated here. Many were sold off to Boston and other places and registered elsewhere.

26 Bill from John Winthrop, Ezra Weston I Papers, folder "EW 1795-1796."

27 Indenture, Ezra Weston I Papers, folder "Legal Matters."

28 John Bradford, "A Vanished Industry: Some Reminiscences of Ship Building in Duxbury, Half a Century Ago," *Old Colony Memorial*, June 1, 1895.

29 Ibid.

30 For various consumers of Weston cordage, see memoranda of cordage and bills, Ezra Weston I Papers, folder "EW undated;" see also Ezra Weston II's Blackbook, "Weston Collection." the archives of the Duxbury Rural and Historical Society, Box 3, entries June 25, 1839 and October 3, 1835, among others.

31 As transcribed in Edmund B. Weston, *In Memoriam: Hon. Gershom Bradford Weston and Deborah Brownell Weston* (Published by Edmund B. Weston, 1916), p. 14.

32 *Records of the Plymouth County Court of General Sessions*, vol. 5, p. 225 as transcribed in David Thomas Konig, ed., *Plymouth County Court Records 1686-1859*, cd-rom published by the New England Historic Genealogical Society and the Pilgrim Society, 2002. See also, *Duxbury Town Meeting Records*, 1800-1803, Office of the Duxbury Town Clerk, pp. 183-190.

33 *Duxbury Town Meeting Records*, Meeting October 13, 1801, p. 185.

34 Justin Winsor, *History of Duxbury*, pp. 19-20.

35 Ibid.

Chapter Three: *E. Weston & Son*

1 Ezra Weston III [sic], "The Weston Family of Duxbury," special collections of the New England Historic Genealogical Society, p. 150.

2 Samuel Eliot Morison, *Maritime History of Massachusetts* (Boston: Houghton Mifflin, 1961), p. 112.

3 Ezra Weston I to Arthur Howland, as quoted in Gershom Bradford, *In With the Sea Wind* (Barre: Barre Gazette, 1962), p. 30.

4 "Hon. Gershom B. Weston of Duxbury," clipping, "Weston" vertical file, archives of the Duxbury Rural and Historical Society. Unfortunately, the source of this clipping cannot be determined. It appears to have been written while Gershom B. Weston, Ezra II's eldest son, was still alive, sometime between 1842 and 1869.

5 Ezra Weston & Son to Captain Reuben Young, July 18, 1800, Ezra Weston I Papers, archives of the Duxbury Rural and Historical Society, folder "Schooner Sophia."

6 Samuel Eliot Morison, *Maritime History of Massachusetts*, p. 73.

7 Gershom Bradford, *In With the Sea Wind* (Barre: Barre Gazette, 1962), pp. 41-46.

8 Ibid.

9 Edmund B. Weston, *In Memoriam: Hon. Gershom Bradford Weston and Deborah Brownell Weston* (Published by Edmund B. Weston, 1916), p. 40.

10 Captain Smith's testimony is given in the *Newburyport Herald*, March 24, 1812; Iss. 102, p. 1.

11 Ibid.

12 Ibid.

13 *Journal of the House of Representatives of the United States of America*, April 22-25, 1812, as transcribed on the Library of Congress, "American Memory" website, http://memory.loc.gov/ammem/amlaw/lwhj.html

14 Ezra Weston's Black Book, "Weston Collection," archives of the Duxbury Rural and Historical Society, Box 4.

15 Edmund B. Weston, *In Memoriam*, p. 40.

16 Ibid., p. 11.

17 Justin Winsor, *History of Duxbury*, p. 165.

18 Data compiled from *Ship Registers of the District of Plymouth, Massachusetts, 1789-1908* (National Archives Project, 1939); E. Weston's Vessel Memorandum Book; E. Weston Cargo Book, "Weston Collection," Box 4; list of vessels compiled by Alden B. Weston, II, "Weston Collection," Box 13.

19 Ibid., p. 164. On Scituate, see L. Vernon Briggs, *History of Shipbuilding on the North River*, (Boston: Coburn Brothers, 1889), p. 110.

20 Samuel Eliot Morison, *Maritime History of Massachusetts*, p. 196.

21 Justin Winsor, *History of Duxbury*, p. 161.

22 Ibid., p. 163.

23 Ibid.

24 Katherine Pillsbury, "The Westons: Duxbury's Caesars," in *The Duxbury Book* (Duxbury Rural and Historical Society, 1987), p. 63.

25 Brig Globe documents, "Weston Collection," Box 5. See also E. Weston's Vessel Memorandum Book," Weston Collection," Box 4.

26 Data compiled from *Ship Registers of the District of Plymouth, Massachusetts 1789-1908*. During the era represented, the Jackson family business consisted primarily of Thomas Jackson and his sons Charles, Thomas, Jr., and William. The Drew Family consisted primarily of Sylvanus Drew and his sons Charles and Reuben.

27 Sylvanus Sampson to Ezra Weston II, n.d., Ezra Weston I Papers, archives of the Duxbury Rural and Historical Society, folder "Estate."

28 Ezra Weston Sampson to Sylvanus Sampson, March 29, 1823, Ezra Weston I Papers, folder "Estate."

29 Ezra Weston II to Sylvanus Sampson, March 25, 1823, Ezra Weston I Papers, folder "Estate."

30 Numerous economic indicators are used to determine the relative value of money over time. The unskilled wage rate is here used because it provides a good indication of the wealth accumulated by the Westons based on today's salaries. The conversions were obtained through *Economic History Services*, "What is the Relative Value in U.S. Dollars?" http://eh.net/hmit/compare/.

32 Compilation of various inventories, Ezra Weston I Papers, folder "Estate."

33 Unsigned note, n.d., Ezra Weston I Papers, folder "Estate."

Chapter Four: *The House*

1 Edmund B. Weston, *In Memoriam: Hon. Gershom Bradford Weston and Deborah Brownell Weston* (Published by Edmund B. Weston, 1916), pp. 19 and 30.

2 Justin Winsor, *History of Duxbury*, p. 125.

3 Although it is often confusing to refer to the son of Ezra II as Ezra IV, it is so done to distinguish him from his older brother who died young. In actuality, Ezra IV referred to himself as Ezra Weston, Jr. To use this appellation here would simply make a confusing situation more so.

4 Ezra Weston III [sic], "The Weston Family of Duxbury," special collections of the New England Historic Genealogical Society, p. 153.

5 Lucia Knapp Royall, "King Caesar House," "Weston Collection," archives of the Duxbury Rural and Historical Society, Box 8, p. 6.

6 Lucia Bradford to Elizabeth Bradford, "Weston Collection," Box 8.

7 Samuel Eliot Morison, *Maritime History of Massachusetts* (Boston: Houghton Mifflin, 1961), pp. 187-190.

8 Letter from the Town of Duxbury to President Thomas Jefferson, 1808, as quoted in Katherine Pillsbury, "Sea and Shore," in *The Duxbury Book* (Duxbury Rural and Historical Society, 1987), p. 51.

9 Samuel Eliot Morison, *Maritime History of Massachusetts*, p. 191.

10 Information on the moving of Weston wharf buildings taken from a letter from Dr. Reuben Peterson to Ellen Bradford Stebbins, October 2, 1939, "Weston Collection," Box 8. Peterson was researching the whereabouts of the various buildings.

11 *Old Colony Memorial*, November 23, 1938.

12 Frederick B. Knapp, Journal 1886, archives of the Duxbury Rural and Historical Society.

13 Lucia Knapp Royall, "King Caesar House," p. 2.

Chapter 5: *A Reformation*

1 Samuel Eliot Morison, *Maritime History of Massachusetts* (Boston: Houghton Mifflin Company, 1961), p. 97.

2 Ezra Weston, III [sic] "Weston Family of Duxbury, Mass,," Special Collections of the New England Historic Genealogical Society, p. 170.

3 *Boston City Directories* 1822-1840 (Charles Stimpson, publisher).

4 Ezra Weston's Black Book, "Weston Collection," archives of the Duxbury Rural and Historical Society, Box 4. See also Edmund B. Weston, *In Memoriam: Hon. Gershom Bradford Weston and Deborah Brownell Weston* (Published by Edmund B. Weston, 1916), p. 31.

5 Ezra Weston's Black Book. See also Boston City Directories, 1825-1830.

6 William S. Rossiter, *Days and Ways in Old Boston* (Boston: State Street Trust Company, 1915), p. 44.

7 L. Vernon Briggs, *History of Shipbuilding on the North River* (Boston: Coburn Brothers, 1889), pp. 227-233.

8 New Bedford Whaling Museum website, http://www.whalingmuseum.org/exhibits/lagoda.html

9 L. Vernon Briggs, *History of Shipbuilding on the North River*, p. 356.

10 The *Boston Gazette*, quoted in the *Baltimore Patriot*; October 31, 1831; Issue 94, p. 2

11 Ezra Weston to Captain Seth F. Sprague, letter dated September 6, 1833, "Weston Collection," archives of the Duxbury Rural and Historical Society, Box 6.

12 John Bradford, "A Vanished Industry," *Old Colony Memorial*, June 1, 1895.

13 "The Surprise," http://www.eraoftheclipperships.com/page17web3.html

14 Ichabod Simmons, Log Book of the Brig Levant, "Weston Collection," archives of the Duxbury Rural and Historical Society, Box 5.

15 Laurence Bradford, *Historic Duxbury* (Boston: Fish Printing, 1900), p. 88.

16 Data primarily from Ezra Weston Vessel Memorandum Book, "Weston Collection," archives of the Duxbury Rural and Historical Society, Box 4. See also *Ship Registers of the District of Plymouth, Massachusetts 1789-1908* (National Archives Project, 1939). Notations regarding masters of vessels in the Vessel Memorandum Book are generally well kept but not always complete. Note that some dates on this table are approximations. Also, it is possible that tours of duty for certain masters were not noted and therefore there are other names that might appear in this table. The purpose, however, is to indicate some of the key figures during the late period of the firm—those master mariners who served five or more years on board Weston vessels.

17 Letters from "E. Weston & Sons" to Captain David Cushman, April-May 1842, "Cushman Papers," archives of the Duxbury Rural and Historical Society, folder "Ship *Undine* letters."

18 Lucie Hall Cushman, "Cushman Family History," p. 3, manuscript in the Cushman Papers, archives of the Duxbury Rural and Historical Society, Box 4.

Chapter Six: *The Late Fleet*

1 Arthur J. Rolnick, Bruce D. Smith, and Warren E. Weber, "The Suffolk Bank and the Panic of 1837: How a Private Bank Acted as a Lender-of-Last-Resort" http://www.imes.boj.or.jp/cbrc/cbrc-24.pdf

2 Ezra Weston, Black Book, "Weston Collection," archives of the Duxbury Rural and Historical Society, Box 4. See also letter from Thomas Herrick to Martin Waterman, 2/8/1838, "Waterman Papers," archives of the Duxbury Rural and Historical Society, folder 1.

3 Letter from Captain Josiah Knowles to Captain David Cushman, "Cushman Papers," archives of the Duxbury Rural and Historical Society, folder "Ship *Undine* Letters."

4 *Old Colony Memorial*, April 3, 1838.

5 Letter from Charles Palmer to Captain David Cushman, June 8, 1842 "Cushman Papers," archives of the Duxbury Rural and Historical Society, folder "Ship *Undine* Letters."

6 Letter from E. Weston & Sons to David Cushman, April 28, 1843 "Cushman Papers," archives of the Duxbury Rural and Historical Society, folder "Ship *Undine* Letters."

7 *Old Colony Memorial*, May 29, 1841.

8 Plymouth County Registry of Deeds, Book 211, Page 23.

9 Dispatches from the American Consul in Liverpool 1845, National Archives and Records administration. Port entries for the latter half of that year show that only 12 vessels involved in the Liverpool cotton trade, all registered in New York City, were larger than the *Hope*.

10 John Bradford, "A Vanished Industry," *Old Colony Memorial*, June 1, 1895.

11 Ibid.

12 For data on American trade in Smyrna, I am much indebted to Rebecca Robinson who conducted and shared a tabulation of the reports on port entries in the Dispatches from American Consuls in Smyrna at the National Archives. It should be noted that in calculating the percentage of arrivals 1823-1829, four of the vessels belonging to Weston were marked in consular reports as registered in Boston. Here they have been included in the 10% figure belonging to Duxbury.

13 Dispatches from American Consuls in Smyrna, 1823-1829, National Archives and Records Administration. Information on the opium trade is taken from Charles C. Stelle, "American Trade in Opium to China, 1821-39," *Pacific Historical Review*, v. 16: March 1941.

14 Information on the trade patterns of Weston vessels are taken from tabulations of "Ezra Weston's Vessel Memorandum Book" and the "Weston Cargo Book" kept by Alden B. Weston, "Weston Collection," archives of the Duxbury Rural and Historical Society, Box 4. These two books are the most important surviving records of the Weston firm. The former lists the arrivals and departures of the Weston fleet from 1830 to 1857 (some 1,200 port-to-port voyages in all). The latter contains cargo manifests for Weston vessels from 1836 to 1846.

15 Ellen Bradford Stebbins, "A Home on the Rolling Deep: Capt. John Bradford Seen through Journals, Letters and the Mists of Memory," manuscript, archives of the Duxbury Rural and Historical Society, p. 2.

16 Robert G. Albion, William A. Baker, and Benjamin W. Labaree, ed., *America and the Sea: A Maritime History* (Mystic, CT: Mystic Seaport, Inc., 1998), p. 318. *Handbook of Texas Online*, s.v. "Screwman's Benevolent Association,"

17 Regarding the record breaking cargo, see John Bradford, "A Vanished Industry: Some Reminiscences of Ship Building in Duxbury," *Old Colony Memorial*, June 1, 1895. For data on vessels entering Liverpool, see Dispatches from the American Consul at Liverpool, 1845, National Archives and Records Administration.

18 Kent Diary, 1845, archives of the Duxbury Rural and Historical Society.

19 Ibid.

20 Ibid.

21 Dispatches from the American Consul at Liverpool, 1845, National Archives and Records Administration.

22 Paul B. Pixton, "The Tyrian and Its Mormon Passengers," Mormon Historical Studies, Spring 2004, Mormon Historical Sites Foundation, Salt Lake City, UT.

23 "Ezra Weston's Vessel Memorandum Book," in the "Weston Collection," archives of the Duxbury Rural and Historical Society, box 4.

24 Excerpts from Osbon's memoirs are taken from a typewritten copy in the Edward Harvey Sampson Scrapbook, "Illustrative Section," archives of the Duxbury Rural and Historical Society.

25 Ibid.

26 Ibid.

27 Bradley Osbon to Edward Harvey Sampson, Edward Harvey Sampson Scrapbook, archives of the Duxbury Rural and Historical Society.

28 Massachusetts Death Records, Massachusetts Archives, v. 3, p. 66.

29 *Old Colony Memorial*, August 20, 1842.

30 *Old Colony Memorial*, August 27, 1842.

Chapter Seven: *The Sons*

1 Edmund Weston, *In Memoriam: Hon. Gershom Bradford Weston and Deborah Brownell Weston* (Published by Edmund Weston, 1916), p. 59.

2 Ezra Weston, Vessel Memorandum Book, "Weston Collection," archives of the Duxbury Rural and Historical Society, Box 4.

3 "Ezra Weston's Vessel Memorandum Book," section on the *Magnet*, "Weston Collection," Box 4, archives of the Duxbury Rural and Historical Society.

4 This discussion is recounted in Gershom Weston's own words in *Reply of a Committee*, published by the First Parish Church, 1851, archives of the Duxbury Rural and Historical Society, p. 23.

5 Edmund Weston, In Memoriam, p. 20.

6 Ibid., p. 24

7 Letters from various Duxbury soldiers to Gershom B. Weston, "Weston Collection," archives of the Duxbury Rural and Historical Society, Box 13.

8 Edmund Weston, In Memoriam, p. 37.

9 Mrs. John Bradford, "The Burning of the Residence of Mr. Gershom Weston in Duxbury," unpublished manuscript, archives of the Duxbury Rural and Historical Society, April 8, 1850.

10 Mary Livermore, *The Story of My Life* (Hartford, CT: A. D. Worthington & Co., Publishers, 1899), p. 374.

11 Gershom Weston, *Reply of a Committee*, p. 24.

12 Ibid., p. 20-26

13 Ezra Weston II, "Ezra Weston's Black Book," archives of the Duxbury Rural and Historical Society, Box 4.

14 Ezra Weston, Jr. [sic] "An Address Delivered before the Massachusetts Horticultural Society," (Boston: Tuttle, Weeks & Dennett, 1836), pp. 6-7.

15 This poem of unspecified authorship is taken from William Bradford Weston, *Hon. Seth Sprague of Plymouth County* (Milton: Published by William Bradford Weston, 1915), preface. William B. Weston (1830-1915) was a grandson of Ezra Weston II.

16 Ezra and Alden Weston to Captain Seth Sprague, Seth F. Sprague Papers, archives of the Duxbury Rural and Historical Society.

17 Edmund Weston, *In Memoriam*, p. 66.

18 Ibid., p. 66.

19 *Old Colony Memorial*, May 19, 1865.

20 United States Censuses, 1870 and 1880.

21 John Bradford, "A Vanished Industry," *Old Colony Memorial*, June 1, 1895. E. Waldo Long, *The Story of Duxbury 1637-1937* (Duxbury, MA: The Duxbury Tercentenary Committee, 1937), p. 108.

Epilogue: *The Legacy*

1 Duxbury Clipper, April 29, 1965, p. 1.